MOVEMENT & DANCE
EDUCATION

Movement & Dance Education

Marion North
Director, Laban Centre for Movement & Dance

Northcote House

First published by Maurice Temple Smith Ltd in 1973
Reprinted 1990

British Library Cataloguing in Publication Data
North, Marion
  [Movement education]. Movement and dance education.
  1. Schools. Curriculum subjects: Physical education
  I. [Movement education] II. Title
  613.707′1

ISBN 0-7463-0534-6

Reprinted in 1990 by Northcote House Publishers Ltd, Plymbridge House,
Estover Road, Plymouth PL6 7PZ, United Kingdom. Tel: Plymouth (0752)
705251. Telex: 45635. Fax: (0752) 777603.

Printed and bound in Great Britain by BPCC Wheatons Ltd, Exeter

I The Practice of Movement Teaching

II Compositions for the Junior and Middle School

III Understanding Children through observing their Movement

Four aspects of movement
(a) The body
(b) Effort
Phrases
The elements of movement
Summary of the elements of movement
Ability to alternate between opposite attitudes
Combinations of three elements appearing at the same time
Combination of two elements appearing at the same time
(c) Spatial directions and patterns
Placement of shapes
Planes of movement
Levels of space which are used by an individual
(d) Relationships

Mary: aged seven
Introduction
Body aspects
Effort
Conclusion
Response to different materials
Space
Penny and Jean: twins, aged twelve plus
General background
Body aspects
Effort
Space
Relationships
Andrew: aged twelve plus
General background
Body aspects
Effort
Space
Relationships
Jimmy: aged eight
Conclusions

I The Practice of Movement Teaching

1 *What is Movement Education?*

'Movement education' is not just a new piece of educational jargon or a pedantic change of name for 'physical education' or 'PE'. The term 'movement' covers a far wider field of study, although it is fair to say that some teachers of 'physical education' have tried to stretch the term to include aspects of education beyond traditional sports, games, gymnastics, and dance. In my opinion the terms 'movement' and 'movement studies' are more comprehensive and meaningful expressions for the study of the whole field of human movement, and of the ways in which movement both develops and expresses the inner lives of children and their relationships with other people. Only one area in this entire field could properly be called 'physical education'. (The London Institute of Education has in fact adopted the terms 'movement' and 'movement studies'.)

Movement education in the school setting, therefore, covers those aspects of 'movement' or 'movement studies' which are relevant to children and young people, either in the classroom and the set lesson in the hall or gymnasium or outdoors, or in sports, games and so on which do not form part of the school timetable. If the impression is given by this that no more is meant than activity lessons of one kind or another, there would indeed be little difference between the new concept and the old-style PE lesson. In fact, the greatest difference probably lies in the change of attitude, outlook and understanding of the teachers or leaders.

Education through movement, or movement education?

The type of question posed in this heading is familiar in all the disciplines which are a part of school life. The concept behind such questions is familiar in the sphere of art, for example, as 'education through art', but it is equally relevant to all school subjects. Certainly movement, particularly movement which can be considered as an art-form, gives a direct, bodily medium through which a child's development as an individual within the group may flourish. Equally, experience and practice of movement, in the skill of handling material, in developing agility and in the self-mastery of the body in dramatic and dance activities—that is, education *in* movement—can be recognised as valuable in its own right.

What kind of movement 'mastery' is appropriate
for children?

There are two kinds of human movement which are vital to all people.

The first type consists of the rhythms and patterns of movement made by someone's body. There are the variations in his stance, for instance, or the static tensions in different areas of his body—stiff neck, drooping shoulders, tensely poised head, elbows held tightly against the sides, and so on. The fleeting expressions on his face are other examples of these patterns, and so are his gait, the gestures he uses when speaking, and so on. These are our 'personal' movement patterns, many of them so persistent that they are recognised as characteristics of our personality. Other patterns of movement are more temporary, and reveal only the mood of the moment, arising from a particular situation.

This kind of movement serves no practical or functional purpose, but reflects an inner state of mind and feeling. It can be said that the body 'speaks', both in what it is seen to do and in how it does it; a child who is shy and timid will not stand upright, 'open', with head lifted, eyes raised, and body at ease. He is more likely to be 'withdrawn', that is, pulling back parts of his body, with head dropped forward and down, and his shoulders narrowed, often with hands clutching at a part of himself or fists tightly clasped. His legs may be touching, his toes turned inwards, the whole body having many 'counter tensions' in it. A child who is excited, happy and exuberant will not only hold his body differently from the shy child, but will show in his rhythmic patterns and 'phrases' many sudden small repetitive movements, like vibrations.

Older children and adults gradually learn to hide these obvious patterns, but in subtle ways—facial expressions, shoulder shrugs, toe tappings—they reveal the inner bodily states of excitement, annoyance, placidity, fear, agitation, and so on. Those states of mind (and corresponding body movements) which are habitual to us, leave their mark in typical postures, gestures, facial expressions, and the like.

The second type of human movement is concerned with 'functional activity', that is, movement directed to a practical or external purpose—doing a job, manipulating materials, climbing a gate, responding to some external material challenge. This kind of skill varies from the crudest manipulative ability to the most subtle and sensitive, from the clumsy and awkward to the agile and graceful. It is to this physical skill and functional activity that the physical educators contribute most. Even in 'dance', much of the work is no more than carefully learning patterns of steps, and there are few teachers of folk and national dance who have managed to help the children to use such skills in the service of an inner or artistic experience.

Although it is possible to recognise these two kinds of movement function, the first serving mainly an inner purpose and the second an outer purpose, in practice the two often appear together. The more skilful and automatic the functional movement, the greater the degree of personal variation. Equally, the first steps in learning any skill (for instance, learning to write or to throw a ball) are often accompanied by considerable movement expressive of intense concentration, and often cramp and anxiety.

A knowledge of human movement can help the teacher to distinguish subtle aspects of the child's movement patterns. He (or she)[1] need no longer generalise: 'He is very awkward and clumsy' or 'She is very dainty and sensitive' or 'She is unable to handle material without spoiling it' or 'He is able to make very delicate objects'. The teacher who has a greater awareness of the possible ranges of human movement, a recognition of personal patterns and rhythms, will be able to make more appropriate responses to the child.

[1] Throughout the rest of the book, the teacher is referred to as 'he', for the sake of simplicity.

'Appropriate responses' and 'appropriately initiated movement' are phrases which briefly summarise the good teacher's relation to the children. But what is appropriate? The teacher must know what movement children are capable of: even more importantly, he must understand its significance through his own personal experience. Here is the central notion of movement education, that a teacher who is himself sensitively aware and alive in his own body is better able both to respond to the child's approach and to choose appropriate challenges for the child. This intuitive, aware, alive response must be related to a knowledge and understanding of movement itself. So the mastery we consider 'appropriate' is, for the teacher, self-knowledge and awareness through experience and observation; and for the children, mastery not only of skills and agilities but also of a wide range of body 'vocabulary' and a recognition of the *meaning* of movement.

What is the 'vocabulary' of movement?

The meaning of the word 'vocabulary' in movement is similar to its usual meaning in language. Movement occurs in 'phrases' and 'sentences', just as do speech and song. Each phrase or sentence is made up of different movement 'words', whose significance is related to the 'words' that have gone before, and those that follow.

For example, in the art of movement, a 'sentence' or 'phrase' or 'motif' might be chosen to express the idea of folding away, retreating into oneself, cutting oneself off from the rest of humanity. Each part of such a phrase will be chosen because of the precise meaning required. If this withdrawal is reluctant and resisting, there will be qualities of restraint: different parts of the body may be in opposition and the timing may be sustained or interrupted. If the reluctance decreases, the movement will become less tense, less inhibited, and calmer as the body 'closes'; if the reluctance grows, the reverse will happen. The choice of this motif and its meaning determines what will follow. If the reluctance grows considerably, the inner tension may so build up that the body is hard and cramped as the limbs close in on themselves, and only an 'explosion' or sudden revolt in the body moves it into the next phrase or sentence. On the other hand, a peaceful ending to a withdrawing phrase may lead into a gentle and poised movement, perhaps involving turning (to emphasise the inwardness), or stepping, or sinking; the next phrase may then develop as a new and independent movement.

Every phrase in movement is chosen, as words are chosen in poetry, to say as precisely as possible what is meant. One must consider which part of the body can best make the statement. Is a movement of the whole body needed, or one involving the upper part of the body or perhaps only the eyes, or fingers, or shoulders? Does the body travel through space, or turn, or lift, or sink, or close, or open out?

As pointed out already, the chosen rhythm, accent and quality of the phrase will depend on its meaning. So one must ask oneself whether the phrase should be lively, urgent and exciting; boisterous or calm; forceful and dominating or weak and yielding; devious or straightforward; easy or restrained. Does a phrase start by expressing one mood and finish in a new mood? Has it a regular pattern, like a regular musical phrase, or is it irregular and more like a speech rhythm? Again, how is the body moving in space? Is it flying upwards, or retreating, or edging sideways, or drooping to the floor, or moving forwards in attack? Is the amount of space used intended to impose restrictions on the body, or can the movement be free and expansive and spreading?

Another consideration is whether or not the child is moving together with, or in relation to, others: is he alone, isolated and unconscious of others, or is he moving together with a partner, a small group or a large group?

Summarising briefly, in considering the vocabulary of movement one must take into account

(a) the body and the most appropriate parts to use;

(b) the way of moving, its rhythm and quality (in phrases);

(c) where the movement takes place;

(d) with whom the movement takes place.

If the movement phrase is to serve an 'inner' rather than an 'outer' function, and is therefore part of a composed sequence of phrases, like a poem or song, the choice will depend on the precise meaning of the phrase and its place within the whole movement 'poem'. It follows that the vague meandering which is often mistaken for movement, and which is likely to be the response to the suggestion 'Move how you like to the music', has no more place in a formulated programme of movement education than the making of random noises has to do with musical education. (It is a pity that this kind of suggestion is sometimes made in the BBC's programme, *Music and Movement*.)

If the movement is to serve an 'outer' or functional purpose, the selection of movement will not be made for its meaning, but rather for its efficiency. This is essentially an ability to manoeuvre around and over objects skilfully and with agility. Such movement is not a matter of expression but of manipulation of the body. For example, successfully hitting a ball means moving into the most appropriate position at the correct time and employing the most efficient body action. Both the action and the use of the body give pleasure and exhilaration, and it is generally recognised that the greater our skill, the greater is the satisfaction and feeling of well-being we enjoy.

What is the difference between movement phrases in a movement composition and in a practical situation?

Again, we can compare the use of language as a practical and functional tool, and language used poetically.

The choice of movement vocabulary is different for each of the two uses. For the former, it will be skilful agility; for the latter *meaning*. Perhaps the best way of approaching the topic of meaning is to realise that movements, like words and sentences in a poem, become carriers of symbolic expression, encompassing more than description can convey, and so 'speaking' directly and symbolically. This should not be confused with mimed language, which is not symbolic but uses the sign to stand in for the word so that if you know the key you can interpret: symbols are different from signs in that they cannot be equated with a single word or meaning. In both poetry and dance it is important to remember that the actual words or movements are not symbolic in themselves, but only in their particular use in the context.

Many children begin to use movement symbolically long

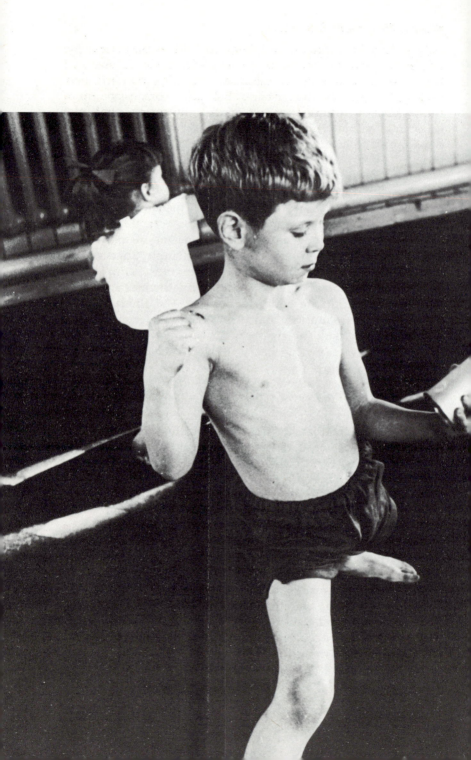

before they are conscious of doing so, just as they make use of colour and pattern and sound and words. A teacher's laboured explanations of symbolic meaning are not only useless, but actually reveal his own lack of understanding of the symbol. The teacher rather needs to be aware at a deeper level and to recognise and accept and show a sensitive response in his teaching.

Should children be 'taught' movement vocabulary first, so that they can use it later in the service of a skill or art?

It is a mistake to think that children in the primary school have 'not done any movement'. Students often believe that they are starting with an entirely 'empty' child, but this is far from the truth. By being alive, a child must already have mastered a rich range of movements. The normal child of five has developed incredible skills of agility, manual dexterity and body manipulation. Just think, for example, of his learning to stand upright and to walk; the child is a natural movement practitioner. His body already speaks clearly and concisely for him, much more so than his actual speech, and he is a most keen and responsive observer of movement. He does not need telling when someone is sympathetic towards him, or when someone is angry, or rejecting, or anxious. The child responds to adults and other children in his own personal way. In addition he can already sense how to arouse sympathy in others, or how to create anxiety; and he can often manoeuvre a situation to his advantage.

The teacher, then, must
  (a) help the children retain their range and 'mastery'; and
  (b) help them to develop it in a way that is appropriate to their general growth.

Without doubt, forcing children to sit still at their desks all day did not help this development, but it is also questionable whether the total restlessness and lack of purposeful centring of interest found in the less efficient schools in the old 'free' days was very effective either!

Given reasonable access to materials, most children will enjoy exercising their skills, whether within the classroom, on agility apparatus, or in the playground. Teachers who are afraid to ask for repetition and to expect improvement should watch the natural persistence of young children in mastering a skill. Nevertheless, leaving children alone with material is not enough. Although too much hastening or 'over-teaching' will have a negative result, the teacher does have a positive part to play in aiding the children's development. In the sections in this book on practical agility and small-apparatus work, suggestions will be made for suitable themes and challenges both for the class and individuals. As long as the teacher retains his sensitivity, he can encourage and support; then, when necessary, he can step back. It is crucial that he is able to recognise when to remain silent, when to help by consolation or praise, and even when to say 'No'.

The good teacher will realise that a child's improvement in a particular skill or agility is achieved by practising those movements themselves, and not from isolated movement practice. The skills are learned in phrases—just as speech is heard in phrases, long before words are isolated. At first, the phrases and sentences may be short and the skills limited. For instance, the child might mount one step of a flight of steps and jump down. But prolonged practice of bending the knee in order to transfer the weight for stepping later, would be worse than useless. We learn in wholes, not in isolated parts. A child would not learn language if he heard only single words until he had enough words to make sentences. He would never learn music if he heard only single notes. He knows a tune long before he knows notes. He knows sentences before letters. In the same way, the child knows whole actions before parts.

This is not to say that, when he has virtually mastered the whole, the child may not, at the right time, benefit from some practice of parts—provided they are related to the whole. For instance, though he should first be allowed to hold a bat in any way he likes, to get the 'feel' of it, it would be helpful later to make suggestions for improving his grip, stance, swing, and so on.

If we turn to movement as an art-form, the same principle is valid. 'I am growing out of the ground, and it's very hard so I have to push, and I burst out and roll away into a little ball, then . . .' The child will know a great deal about what is involved in this kind of action long before he can practice an isolated movement of pushing with different parts of his body in many directions. Indeed it is questionable whether such isolated actions are ever of much use, if the aim is towards meaningful movement. It is far better to work from the phrases and sequences, and what is being said, than to practise meaningless actions.

Not that all movement need have a story. The pure joy of movement for its own sake is exciting and absorbing, provided it is truly a matter of movement phrases, not physical contortions. This is true even of simple movement phrases: hands creeping out from close to the body 'as if they were looking for something' and 'jumping back to safety'; or the body becoming 'a huge prickly creature that is spiky and jumps from one place to the next'; or closing the eyes and quietly breathing, gradually expanding the chest further with each breath and then letting out the air with a hissing noise; or whirling 'like a top and toppling over, or stopping just in time'; or two children facing each other, keeping exactly in time as they grow from the ground higher and higher, and then drop to the floor. All of these are whole movement phrases, not isolated elements or aspects of movement. They are real and alive. Many ideas can be taken from watching the spontaneous movements of children and of other living things, and movements in nature generally, such as the curling of smoke or the scattering of material in an explosion.

At all stages, but especially in the infant school, it is important to work from wholes to parts, just as, when one is teaching a song or a poem, the whole is presented first and the parts looked at later in order to deepen the study. Also, the teacher must present the parts in their context and not in isolation. In the junior school, although the children have progressed to whole movement sequences, longer sentences and paragraphs, the principle is the same. If the teacher asks for too many exploratory actions and isolated ('babyish') phrases, the children lose interest. No matter whether they have done it before; let them enjoy whole compositions, rituals, dances, and dramatic sequences which are full of action and imagination, and they will gladly practise parts later to make the composition say more clearly what is intended.

Is there a 'basic' movement which is applicable to all kinds of movement?

In expressive movement, there is no such thing as 'basic' movement, although this term has been used by some people. There are, of course, common elements in movement which can be defined, but 'basic' implies a limited range of movements, like classical steps or gestures which can be organised in various ways. Just as there is no 'basic' language, in this sense, there is no 'basic' movement. The meaning of a movement phrase changes according to its placing in relation to other phrases or pauses, and according to the situation and the person.

Summary

The teacher in the primary school, who is concerned with the all-round growth and development of the children, will of necessity be interested in and responsible for their movement development. General development and movement development belong together and neither is possible without the other. The teacher's concern will take the form of careful observation of the children, whether by using his intuition or by a consciously developed skill in all situations of school life, as well as in the movement lessons. (This kind of observation is dealt with in Part Three.) The teacher will also learn to recognise how the children's own sensitivity and awareness of themselves and others can be heightened through their experience of movement, and their recognition of movement, rhythm, pattern and form in all aspects of their lives and environment.

2 Movement Lessons in School

How can the time allocated to movement be used best?

If we agree that movement education is more than jumping about in a playground or hall, we must also agree that valuable experience in movement can take place at all times in all places. The restrictions and limitations imposed on movement in the classroom are not necessarily bad. It is true that all children, of primary school age find too extreme a limitation on their bodily movement both difficult and damaging, but it is also true that care and concentration on a task involving finely coordinated bodily movements can best be encouraged in a limited space—for example, subtle hand movements, shapes, patterns and rhythms; careful bodily adjustments; facial expressions and the movement involved in making sounds.

Subtleties in mime, or the coordination of the body in small-scale movements, can be achieved by performing plays, by painting or handling clay and other materials, within the classroom. The very restricted use of movement necessary to make marks and patterns on paper (as in drawing, painting or writing on small pieces of paper) encourages precision, care and control which are just as important as carefree, expansive movements. Nevertheless, an opportunity for the freer use of space should be available each day, when the children can move into and through space with fewer restrictions and in a more exuberant and expansive way.

The chief aim of movement education is learning to 'know' one's body, in rhythm, action and stillness, in skills and in striving, in freedom and restriction. This knowledge contributes to a 'sense of self', that is, an awareness of oneself which is intimately bound up with becoming a person in one's own right, or with what psychologists call achieving a 'body image'. Such an image of the self is essential to the

development of our potential as human beings, both as individuals and in our relationship with others.

A knowledge of one's body can best be nurtured through a rich range of movement experiences, the subtle as well as the gross, the vigorous as well as the gentle, and the rhythmical as well as the smooth and controlled. But in all cases these experiences must be genuinely felt in the body and should not be confused with mere physical action. (The difference between 'bodily' and 'physical' movement, a central idea in movement education, will be discussed later.)

It should be clear, therefore, that the actual movement lesson in the hall or playground is only a part of a true education through movement, even though it is a very valuable part and one to which a great deal of this book will be devoted.

The ideas explained in Chapter 1 show that it is reasonable to allocate half of the time available in the hall to movement as an art-form, and half to the more practical aspects of movement. This means that alternate days should be given to the art of movement and to play involving small apparatus, leading to the learning of games or to agilities of climbing and scrambling. If Mondays, say, were given to developing agilities, Tuesdays and Thursdays to the art of movement, Wednesdays to the use of small apparatus, and Fridays to the continuation of any one of these (or for swimming), the children would have a balanced 'diet'. The teacher can only maintain a balance by keeping in mind that the main distinctions are between movement as art, serving mainly an inner function, and practical movement, serving mainly an outer function.

Each of the two major aspects has many sub-divisions. Skills and agilities at the infant stage include

(a) climbing and scrambling on fixed apparatus, such as jumping over and tumbling on to mats, forms or larger pieces of equipment, as well as the skills of balancing on the hands, rolling, jumping, and so on, using the floor itself as the main external 'challenge';

(b) throwing, catching or hitting with small movable pieces of apparatus, such as balls, hoops and bats. The simplest of these skills can soon be developed

into a game with a partner. Children need to practise
the more difficult skills individually before using
them in a game with other children, but they can
use simple skills in this way much earlier. Even
before a child can throw and catch accurately, he
can roll a ball to a partner and field it when it is
returned to him.

In the junior school, the climbing and scrambling mentioned in (a) above have already become skilful agilities, and
the growing physical and mental capacities of the children
enable them to perform increasingly ambitious and subtle
sequences using larger apparatus. Playing with balls, bats,
hoops and so on, as in (b), develops into the physical
expertise of aiming, dribbling, shooting and hitting which
allow more and more complex games to be played successfully with sides, rules and scoring. But it is a pity to launch
the children too early into full-scale adult games, before they
can hope to master either the advanced skills or the complicated rules.

Throughout the primary school, it is evident that children
grow and develop at very different rates, with different gifts,
skills and capacities. These variations comprise not only
differences in learning ability or training, but differences in
capacity for particular kinds of movement patterns and skills.
Even babies exhibit differences of this kind, which appear to
be as much a part of the individual's make-up as the colour of
his hair or eyes. An average class will contain children of such
varied abilities that the teacher must take care to consider the
personal needs of each child.

Lessons devoted to the art of movement aim not so much
at physical skills as at the experience of movement in
sequences which have an inner meaning beyond the giving of
a skilful performance. Such lessons will cover dramatic
action, mime, ritual and rhythmic dance. At the infant stage,
the experience of moving in small phrases in many varied
ways will enrich the child's awareness of movement—for
instance, phrases of buoyancy and stopping, like a ball
bouncing and then stopping; of smooth, even stepping, as if
sliding over a very slippery surface; of explosions from the
body centre, as if the body were being scattered; of returning

to the body centre, when all the parts of the body come back together again; and so on.

These are familiar sensations to a child, and they are linked with experiences in his inner life, creating a kind of 'recall' of earlier kinaesthetic experiences. But these new sensations differ from the early ones, in that the movement is phrased and shaped, whereas the earlier experiences may have occurred without any shape or form at all. Within the form or the rhythm or the phrase, even normally frightening sensations will be contained, and the child will be able to cope with them, often for the first time. For example, the sensation of floating, as if walking on air, and then dropping and falling, is familiar to everyone. A baby experiencing this falling can be terrified, as can a child recalling the experience in dreams or in his actual bodily sensations: mastering the movement and its accompanying sensation within the phrased sequence can help the child to recognise and master the fear. This process is also familiar in children's play, much of which recaptures these early kinaesthetic experiences. This holds true for any bodily movement: the gradually increasing mastery of the body, and the accompanying sense of security, result from making links in this way between previous experiences and present ones, so laying the foundation for meaningful movement to develop later into genuine art.

In the junior school, children move and think in longer phrases and sequences. With the teacher's help they can develop whole 'plays' in movement. These may include dramatic sequences of action and reaction, ritualised plays based on ancient or contemporary myths, rhythmical dances and seasonal festivals, and mimed plays in rhythmical or realistic form. Themes for such 'plays' will be discussed in Part Two.

What is the difference between themes for agility classes and for the art of movement?

The difference of presentation between the practical class and the art-of-movement class is related to the aims of the movement. For instance, a sequence alternating the balance of the body, first on the hands, then on the feet, is a theme for the practical agility class; while a clown dance, in which the clown, to amuse his audience, may balance on his hands, is a theme for the art-of-movement class. The sequences will also be developed differently. The agility sequence will aim first at inventiveness and will develop in a simple progression in which skill and sublety of timing will be important. The clown dance will be phrased, given a rhythm and made repetitive, and then performed as skilfully as possible. The development of the clown dance can best be described as being similar to development in music. A motif is developed in different ways, for instance, in size, in the parts of the body used, in rhythm, and in transferring the expression from one part of the body to another. And just as in music there are variations of volume and rhythm, so in the dance the way the body extends out into space and the intensity of strength and timing will subtly vary.

What is the difference between 'bodily' movement and 'physical' movement?

In this book, the term 'bodily movement', implies a full physical/emotional/mental involvement. Even in dancing, it is possible to recognise the difference between a dancer who is performing with whole body involvement and one who is only executing a series of physical actions. If one observes carefully, it becomes apparent that the second type of dancer, though technically perfect, is limiting himself to a physical movement which leaves out all human warmth and vitality, and with them all the nuances of body rhythms and the 'shadow' movements[1] of the face and the body centre. The movement is merely physical, and rather like a machine going through its motions. Sometimes, for physical practice, this precise machine-like movement can be valuable, particularly for the professional dancer who must aim at achieving the maximum technical skill of which his body is capable, but it has little place in primary-school work.

The distinction between skilful practical actions and expressive movement cannot be over-emphasised. For this reason, I advocate that each session be devoted fully to one

[1] Small, usually involuntary movements, often of face or isolated parts of the body which reflect or 'shadow' inner moods, feelings or attitudes.

kind of movement or the other. The twenty-minute or half-hour lesson is too short for the two to be mixed, and there is confusion if 'outer' and 'inner' functional needs are not clearly distinguished. It is unreasonable for a child to be encouraged to leap on to a box, for instance, and then be asked to unroll and yawn expressively, as if just waking up! The unrolling and yawning belong to a different kind of lesson.

What about team games and sports?

Competitive sports and school teams seem to belong to the club activities of a school, where those boys and girls at the upper end of the junior school choose the particular activity they wish to follow. All children are not, and need not be, interested and involved in competitive sports; and it does seem that, influenced by our public schools as well as by American attitudes towards sports, such activities are over-valued in many schools. Often this preoccupation has been to the detriment of the art of movement. A similar distortion of values has occurred in other areas of education, for instance, the stressing of grammar and the skills of writing, particularly the kind of writing which records events and activities from an external point of view only, while paying mere lip-service to poetry and literature. And just as it is perhaps better to ignore poetry completely than to treat it as a mere exercise in the analysis of language, so the art of movement would be better ignored than reduced to mere physical activity.

Some children need the stimulus to great effort and the consequent satisfaction to be gained from the challenge of team-work and the excellence demanded by competitive sports and games. Other children derive only a sense of failure and rejection from such competition, particularly when competitive sports are over-valued.

What is the relationship between movement and other subjects?

At the primary-school level, the stress should be much more on 'education through movement' than on movement education itself. However, the two are not incompatible, and at this stage the foundations are laid for a movement 'literacy', just as they are for music and the visual arts. The art of movement clearly has many more links with other art-subjects than with games and sports; indeed, the essence of all the arts is the same, however different the media. At the infant and junior level, speech rhythms and sounds, percussion noises and irregular melodic phrases are close to the actual rhythm of movement. Most children spontaneously make sounds and movement together—what are the sounds, if not the movement of special parts of the body becoming audible? A baby often accompanies sounds with movements of its whole body. Young children whoop or yell or hum as they move. The rhythms and patterns of sound and movement are the same. Later the sounds may be more refined, so they do not require total body movement as accompaniment. But any singer or instrumentalist knows that his whole body is totally involved in his singing or playing, while not actively engaged in gross movement. Similarly, even when sounds have become formulated into words and speech patterns, the body will support the meaning through its movements; the intonation, volume and timing of speech are themselves produced by body movements. The body is also still used in gestures, 'shadow' movements, and stance.

Although there is a very close bond between sound and movement, it is not always necessary or desirable to have sound as an accompaniment, stimulus or support. Often a baby moves silently, the rhythms of the body movement itself making a kind of 'silent song'. To the observer who is sensitive to these rhythms, it is like watching a whole orchestra playing. Sometimes the parts of the body move in unison; sometimes the rhythm or time is carried by the arms, then by the trunk, or the legs. At other times the rhythms of different parts of the body overlap, for instance the head and face. Indeed, to write this down, as is possible in movement notation, requires as many lines of rhythm and pattern as an orchestral score.

Not only is sound accompaniment not always necessary, but very often the intrusion of sound, particularly if it is less refined than the movement patterns, will limit the movement rather than enhance it.

Since movement provides its own silent rhythms and

patterns, as well as following sound patterns, it follows that the relationship between the art of movement and music is very close. As the children learn to listen and to distinguish musical sounds, rhythms and patterns, so they can learn to distinguish the patterns and rhythms of their own bodies. This awareness of the 'speech-like' rhythms of the body, which are irregular, can be dulled if the teacher uses regular metrical rhythms too much. But the body carries the regular repetitive rhythms, too. Stepping, walking, running, and jumping provide repetitive rhythmical patterns which are recognisable as having bars of two beats or four beats when the accent is on the same side each time, or three beats when alternating sides are accented. Regular five-rhythms, seven-rhythms, and so on, are a mixture of these accented, repetitive actions. The heartbeat provides the continuous throbbing experience of timing, with increases and decreases of speed and urgency. The body's entire unconscious metabolism is built upon rhythmic sequences which we relate to long before we know about them intellectually.

Rhythm and pattern in music, then, are close to the child's experience of movement. But, although music is traditionally associated with dancing, highly significant parts of the dance may be performed in silence.

The teacher will do well to use this natural relationship, but not to use it exclusively; many things other than music can stimulate a movement response—visual art, patterns, colour, natural happenings, microscopic-cell activity, stories, poems, and so on. Similarly, movement phrases and sequences can be the basis for the making of music.

Movement is related not only to music but also to drama. Drama depends upon the action of the body for its execution, on the body stance, the gestures and the meaningful facial expressions, as well as the intonation of the sounds and words. But drama arises from and is centred around the script and language; and, even in improvised drama, it is the speech, words and verbal expression which should, I believe, carry the action. Otherwise, as happens in too many schools, improvisation is divorced from real drama and is poor movement into the bargain. It was understandable that many drama teachers, confronted with children standing woodenly,

reciting learned lines, flew to the opposite extreme of
'improvisation', using words which did not have to be
learned. Too often, though, the fault was that the children
had nothing of interest to say, or that they did not understand the deeper sense of the poetry or dialogue, concerning
the inner lives of the players. In the absence of this dimension brought by the players, the result will not be drama, in
the sense of being an art-form. Much of the children's
improvisation which is 'organised' at school is at the level of
banal reporting of happenings—we went in a train, and did
this and that—containing little of the content of true drama.
Children who play their own games really 'play'; that is, they
not only enact, but live through an experience, whether it is
cowboys-and-Indians, houses, mothers-and-fathers, hospitals,
or spacemen.

Movement and drama are closely linked, but they are not
the same thing. The sequence of actions in a drama follows
and depends upon the dialogue. Dramatic movement, however, follows a logic of action and movement which depends
upon the rhythm and patterns of individuals or groups and
the way they are related.

Creation in the visual arts depends on the movement of
the whole body. For example, in pottery, the hands alone
mould the clay, but the whole body participates. In painting,
the hand manoeuvres and brush, but it is inspired by the
kinaesthetic bodily sensations already referred to. Visual
shapes and forms and colours capture, as it were, the body's
movement, and stand for themselves, outside the body, as if
they have a life of their own. In this sense, the body serves
the painting or the piece of pottery. Stimulus for movement
can sometimes leap out from a picture or sculpture. Sometimes the children can recognise common elements of rhythm
or shape without being stimulated actually to move. A piece
of music can trigger off an idea for a dance or dramatic
action and lead to an actual movement composition, or it can
stimulate a response and recognition which is not translated
into action.

So this thread of common elements in all the arts can be
recognised: the rhythmical elements; the form and shape; and
the phrasing and wholeness. Each medium speaks for itself

and in its own way, and it is not possible to 'interpret' one art-form as another.

Practical movement activities stand very much in their own right as agilities and skills: there is no convincing evidence that an increase of skill in one area improves skill in another. But there seems little doubt that the more alert and sensitive children become, the more they are aware of capacities, rhythms and gifts of their own bodies, the more generally skilful they will be. Games have traditionally been used as an activity to counter-balance 'brain-work'; but they do, in fact, require judgement, skill, teamwork, and control—all of which are desirable social qualities.

In considering the place of movement within the school curriculum, it must be stressed again that movement can be seen not only as common to all living things, but as giving pattern and form to all aspects of life, both in our inner life and in our environment.

3 The Art-of-Movement Lesson in the Infant School

It is convenient to discuss the earlier primary-school work separately from the later stages. There is, of course, no hard-and-fast division between methods in the infant and junior schools, but the teacher must make the presentation of the work appropriate to the mental, emotional and bodily development of the children. This creates special problems for class teaching in family-grouped schools, and these will be discussed later. The children in the majority of classes have a range of age and development of at least a year, and among them there can be many observable differences in response to the same stimulus.

What is the content of the first lessons?

The content of the lessons at the infant-school stage can be as wide and varied as the gifts of teachers allow. There is, then, no set pattern or form to the lesson, but clear guide-lines can be defined. At this stage, the work is not really 'art', any more than children's paintings and models are in the strict sense 'art', or their music-making 'music'. It is as if in all these activities, the child makes a kind of preliminary exploration of the various media. These explorations help the child to become familiar with the materials of the art; with colours, brushes, clay, drums; and with his own body. They are near to a form of true play. Dr Winnicott[1] suggests that play, in its real sense, together with cultural experiences rooted in tradition, for the core of childhood experience which is the forerunner of true art. Students and teachers should read this paper to gain insight into a view of childhood which will be helpful to their understanding. All children who 'explore the use of materials' (a current cliché

[1] D.W. Winnicott, 'Location of Cultural Experience' in *Playing and Reality*, Tavistock Publication 1971.

in education) are doing a great deal more than improving their skill and mastery of manipulation, although they are doing this too. A child captures, in his early scribbles and drawings, aspects of himself which are or have been inner experiences, or inner kinaesthetic memories and experiences. Rhoda Kellogg has attempted to describe some of these early drawings.[2] Whether or not the detailed descriptions are totally accurate, they clearly reveal the existence of common patterns of development. These patterns must arise from common human experience. They also show that at the early stages of human development, such experience must be primarily of bodily sensations, which the body somehow seems to 'remember'. Similarly, it seems reasonable to assume that certain rhythmic patterns of sound echo within the child and are recognised and remembered by him.

Without doubt, these important sensations of movement in the body, which are not functional in an external sense, and are generally termed 'kinaesthetic' experiences, are not relived as before, but lived again or remembered in a new way which is linked with the earlier experiences. It is when these remembered patterns are touched and awakened and newly experienced that we can claim to be working within the sphere of true movement rather than that of existing functional skills.

Children in their play are remembering all the time. Teachers can help in movement lessons to activate these inner links, and can help the child not only to repeat but to recreate and develop the earlier experiences. As mentioned in Chapter 2, the form of the phrase both clarifies the experience and 'holds' the child securely. It is a mistake to regard movement as a vague indulgence in formless motion, just as it would be to regard music as a formless series of sounds. Music teachers do not mind presenting young children with musical forms, such as nursery rhymes and songs; and I have yet to hear a teacher say to a class 'Make any sounds you like now' and think of the result as music. And yet I have frequently known teachers say in a so-called movement lesson 'Move any way you like', and then wonder why the

[2] R. Kellogg, *What Children Scribble and Why*, National Press, Palo Alto, California, 1955.

result is formless, meaningless and boring, or completely out of hand.

A large space arouses in some children a temptation to move wildly, in others a fear of movement. The teacher must, therefore, have a clear idea of the aim and purpose of a lesson. The presence of forty children in a room having no imposed form or 'structure' provided by desks or apparatus, requires some 'structuring' from the teacher and the children. This structure will be best supplied in one of two ways. A class rhythm can be provided, within which all kinds of variation of movement are possible. Or there can be a challenge of some specific sort, be it an action of the whole body (turning, running and jumping, growing higher and higher) or an action stressing one part of the body (for instance, everyone using the head, or eyes, or spine) or a combination of these. Then the rhythm might be left to the individual child.

How the challenge of the rhythm and its accompanying movement, or the action, is presented is very important. This aspect was touched on in Chapter 2 when one method of giving a challenge was suggested: that is, 'As if . . .'. In writing about movement, words have to stand in their own right, of course, without the intonation and expression added by the voice. This makes it difficult to describe how a sequence can be stimulated almost entirely through the use of the teacher's voice. Saying to a class 'Starting low down, near the ground, and growing higher and higher . . .' in a matter-of-fact, unanimated tone invites an unanimated response. However, by saying it with more sensitive phrasing, with increasing force and rising pitch, there is an immediate 'lighting up' in the children, which in turn brings about their total involvement in the movement. The child can then make the 'As if . . .' for himself.

The use of the expression 'As if . . .' is a particularly valuable one, if it is not used in a limiting way. It can help to link the present experience with a past one, to awaken movement through kinaesthetic memory, and to stimulate the imagination. But the aim should be to awaken *movement* imagination, not visual or verbal imagination. For instance, the suggestion 'Step on tiptoes very gently, as if stepping

carefully on tiny stones, making no sound' stimulates action, whereas 'Step on tiptoes, as if you are a tiny man, or woman, with a red hat and red cloak' stimulates only a visual image. This extreme example is perhaps helpful to indicate that the 'As if . . .' phrase has to be linked with the experience of movement and not another kind of imagery. A similar example of this error was made by a teacher whose class were absorbed in the idea of a long dark passage, which they were to crawl through without being able to see. He asked them: 'What might you do?' The response from one bright six-year-old was 'Switch on your torch'! The dark passage idea was a good one, but totally lost as a stimulus to movement. If the teacher had suggested that the children started by lying, crouching or kneeling on the floor, with eyes closed, as if it was dark and they could not see, so that they used their fingers to feel gently round the floor and into space, forward and backward, they would have used their imagination in a movement way. An immediate link would have been made with all those times they had experienced being in the dark and not knowing what was around them.

How can a teacher become expert in presenting challenges to provoke an inner response?

The teacher must 'think' movement. That is, he must not only think in terms of the intellectual analysis of movement but must have the courage to draw on his own bodily and kinaesthetic experiences. In some adults, a keen sense of movement has somehow remained alive from childhood; but others have sadly neglected this side of life, often because of an almost exclusive development of the intellect. It is almost as though they had cut themselves off from the very roots of their beings.

Today, it is fashionable to say that one can teach movement only if one has received formal training in movement. Of course this is true for those who teach the art of movement to any standard; but it is significant that some of the best primary-school work I have seen has been done by teachers who have had very little experience in movement classes. What they have managed to do is to connect, or reconnect, with their own personal kinaesthetic senses, so that they recognise what the children are doing. They are not being misled by mere agility or inventiveness but are able to sense what is necessary to take the experience further. All of this can be achieved by anyone who has sensitivity and is willing to observe children's movement, though participating in classes of movement obviously helps to develop these attributes.

One word here about the harm which is often done by using, in lieu of a teacher, recorded programmes whose titles imply that they are movement lessons. Usually they are linked with music. The voice suggests an action, or series of actions, to be made 'when the music plays'. Usually these ideas, even if good in themselves, are vaguely presented and emphasised. Worse still, there is no one there to respond to the children and to help develop or sustain their response. The voice then either tells them to repeat the movement, or gives a new stimulus for a new movement. By the time the children have suffered this treatment for some time, they cease to expect any response or development of their movement. They become incapable of working on or developing an idea (and indeed can resent it if it is required) and come to depend on a new outer stimulus for every new movement idea. This is the result of the medium; for real teaching, a teacher is needed. A recorded voice cannot do this, because a person is required, who not only stimulates but responds, sustains, supports and challenges—that is, acts as a human being.

How can a lesson, or series of lessons, be planned?

In planning lessons, the teacher must first outline a possible structure for the lesson and be prepared to make certain challenges and demands of the class. Whatever an experienced class may be able to do alone (or, at some point in their development, with minimum guidance) the young infant classes depend mainly upon the teacher. If they are left to do what they like for a specified half-hour or so, there will be no spontaneous outbreak of creative movement. Many teachers are too afraid that by stimulating, formulating, responding and suggesting, they are imposing on the children and inhibiting spontaneous creation. They appear to expect, unreasonably, that something will happen, if the children are left freely—'Let it come from the child'. Neither poetry, nor music-making, nor drama, nor dance, will grow and develop in this way. If no real teaching is to be done, then it is better to give the children real free time, in the playground, when they can genuinely develop their own plays, rituals, skills, and so on.

A lesson should be planned as a 'partnership'—the teacher being sensitive to the children's needs and responses, and the children having a chance to relate to an adult human being. Of course, at appropriate times, the teacher may properly withdraw and hand over the responsibility for a shorter or longer time to the children, either alone or in groups. The good teacher is aware that children need such independence on occasions, but he also recognises that they need stimulus, response and guidance, again at appropriate times. For the children and teacher alike, unstructured work—the lack of a proper relationship, 'leaving the children to themselves'—can be worse at the early stages than too much order, form and challenge.

The actual movement content of the lessons should be envisaged as a rhythmical whole, rather than as a series of isolated actions or experiences. Sometimes the parts of a lesson will be related by contrast, sometimes by similarity of experiences. For instance, if one has been stimulated to explore and re-experience the world as it appears when one is not upright, but on all fours, or lying on one's side or back, the lesson will rhythmically demand that the experience be contrasted with that of being upright. In such a way, the 'earthboundness' is more anchored, animal-like and focused on the low level, because of inevitable comparison with the relative freedom, uprightness and aspiration of the experience of standing, or growing high, or leaping up into space. By growing up, our field of vision has become radically altered, and with it the balance. To link these two experiences, the early 'downward' focus and the later 'upward' focus, which are contrasted here as opposites, it is possible as a later development to alternate between the two. In other words, one can grow from one state to the other—states of mind as well as states of the body. But, throughout the lessons, it is helpful if the children's attention is drawn to where the movement occurs in the body. This relates to what was earlier described as the development of a 'body image', a sense of the self. This body image, or awareness, arises from inside, rather than outside the body, from the 'feel' of what is happening, as well as from visual observation of it.

Themes for lessons can be developed from any aspect of nature, the environment, the literary, musical and visual arts, or fantasy. The aim is to capture the experience of movement phrases and sequences in the body. At the beginning, the themes will be those best known to children in their fantasy, and practical, lives. Some examples are

flying and floating	:	falling and dropping
rising and growing	:	sinking and shrinking
appearing	:	disappearing
surging and outgoing	:	withdrawing and incoming
whirling and turning	:	holding and stopping
penetrating and piercing	:	surrounding and enfolding
touching	:	leaving
gripping and holding	:	releasing
rubbing and smoothing	:	tearing and breaking
exploding and scattering	:	containing and collecting
exciting and stimulating	:	soothing and calming
vibrating tensely	:	easing tension

All of these occur in the body, or parts of the body, in meaningful phrases. They happen as we travel from one place to another; as we face different directions; as we close our bodies or open them out; as we rise or fall in space.

A lesson can include a number of these experiences of bodily actions, but neither too few nor too many. What is too few? When the children are over-practising them. And too many? When, because of constant change from one to another without sufficient repetition, the children gain no experience. How can you tell what is sufficient? By observing the responses and movements of the children and so recognising their experiences. Ability in this requires practice.

How is the lesson arranged?

The choice of lesson structure is immediately dictated to the teacher by his own preference and by considering the most suitable means to promote or challenge the responses.

Some teachers are more at home, for instance, with voice and words, some with percussion and music. In the end, all teachers will want to extend the range of the work by following up the initial approach with other kinds of stimulus or accompaniment, so that a group of children is not working all the time either with or without music, or percussion, or voice, or in silence.

If a teacher feels more confident in presenting an idea for movement through a dramatic story, then he should do so. Or if he can best support the idea by voice and words, or by using the phrase 'As if . . .', then he should do this. As confidence grows, and experience widens, the teacher will find that there are many approaches and that each one reveals a different subtlety or shade of meaning in the idea. As set down here, the ideas must seem rather undefined, since they are formulated in words which need qualifying if we are to understand them more clearly or try to link them with a real experience. The qualities of the movement itself are far more varied and rich than the words can convey. Is this not what some poetry can do to us, that is to awaken through words the experiences we carry within our bodies? And perhaps more, to extend us through the symbolic use of words to new experiences.

For a simple beginning to a lesson, it is often good to use a unison class rhythm. A simple action is suggested which all can do easily, so that everyone is absorbed and focused in the same movement. This is especially true if there has been much upheaval in getting the children to the hall, changing, walking and stair-climbing. For instance, they might jump together to a phrase of sound on the drum, and stop and crouch down, or bounce like a ball—up and up and up and up and stop! Some teachers prefer the children to be more scattered in the room, practising their own agilities or movement phrases. This can be effective only when the children are fairly confident and experienced.

The contrast between children working on a movement

idea themselves, not seeking any support, and children entirely dependent on the teacher for sustaining the move-ment (as suggested in the jumping) is one which can be used constantly as a theme during a lesson. The first encourages the children to become absorbed in themselves, the second to concentrate on outer sounds and rhythms, as they have to learn to listen to the sounds exactly. By listening with their bodies, not only with their ears, they can begin to anticipate beginnings and endings, accents, rhythmic changes, and so on.

Working with others

From the beginning, young children can learn to be aware of other children's abilities, gifts and differences, as well as their own capacities and bodily feelings. This is encouraged by the teacher directing their observations. Just to say 'Watch John!' does not help much. One is far more likely to focus the children's attention by saying 'Watch John, and see how he makes his body fly out in all directions.' And then 'Watch Mary. Do you see a difference? Perhaps we can all try Mary's way, then try John's way.'

Working together can include the whole class as a massed group, performing a movement phrase such as gradually growing up and up and up and spreading far out—and collapsing down. Individual awareness is often first achieved by having to avoid others as the children weave in and out. To avoid hitting anyone will require twisting, changing speeds, holding back and rushing into spaces.

The children can also work in small groups, and these groups may be quite separate or there may be two groups facing each other. With simple themes, couples can work together, either in opposition, like question-and-answer play, or in unison. For example, rising together, perhaps touching with eyes closed, perhaps not touching but related through looking. Counter-movements are more subtle: for instance, one child may rise as the other sinks, or one may support the weight of the other in pulling or pushing. Dramatic action and reaction can be introduced in simple forms only, until children are very skilled in relating to one another. Although it is true that young children are self-centred and work alone

easily, it is helpful if in each lesson some aspects of the
relationship of one child to the others is included.

Not only do all children love repetition, but repetition is
necessary for experiencing and learning. But the teacher must
be able to sense when it is proper merely to repeat, and when
to repeat with a slight nuance or variation, or when to draw
attention to a special part of the movement—perhaps the part
of the body used, or the rhythm, or the use of space. Within
the plan of a lesson, familiar movement phrases can be
reintroduced at different times for reinforcement, and
certainly they should be carried over from one lesson to
another. It is better to do the movement again straightforwardly, giving the sound or the idea or description, than
to say 'Do you remember what we did yesterday?' and
discuss it at an intellectual level. The intellectual memory is
for the teacher; it comes later for the children.

Each section of the lesson should follow on from the last,
and so the lesson develops as a whole. Much of the material
will be the same as in previous lessons (just as the music
lesson will surely include favourite songs as well as new ones)
but the new lesson should form a new whole, based on the
responses of the children observed during the previous class.
Sometimes a spontaneous idea will arise in the classroom
from either the teacher or the children, and this can be
carried into new 'whole-bodied' movement in the hall.
Alternatively, experiences of movement may stimulate sand
play, or colouring or modelling, when the children return to
the classroom. Often, the movement lesson will be deliberately planned with other subjects and spheres of work in
mind. Such linking helps the children to see how many
aspects of their world are related; for instance, the way that
different kinds of rhythms permeate our inner and external
lives, or how shapes occur in both living and man-made
objects, in our pictures and clay, and in our own bodies when
we move.

The discipline of the art of movement is extremely
demanding, as it would not be if movement's main purpose
were 'letting off steam'. True, 'steam' is released, but it is not
merely 'let off' and wasted; rather it is channelled towards
purposeful and disciplined work. The discipline arises from

the work itself, the striving to achieve a more and more exact meaning from the rhythm, shape and relationships of the moving body—'moving' both in actual motion, and in the stillnesses of inner preparation to move, and the controlled endings after the gross body motion ceases.

What can the teacher do in a system of 'family-grouping'?

The mental, physical and emotional development of children between five and seven years of age covers so wide a range that it would seem impossible to teach such a group of children as one class unit. Indeed, it is doubtful if any teacher confronted with such a situation in a hall could do justice to every child. The best that can be attempted is to make the challenges for movement so varied that different types of children will be able to move appropriately in response to them. If it is at all possible, it might be better to take the younger group of children separately from the older ones, even though this might involve sharing two classes. The very young children normally need a gentler, quieter approach than the exuberant seven-year-olds.

4 The Art-of-Movement Lesson in the Junior School

Discussion of the junior-school programme requires no change of fundamental attitude towards the art of movement. Chapter 3 was concerned with allowing the children experiences of movement which were meaningful to them within the disciplined art-forms of phrases and sequences. Just as there are occasions in the infant's lessons when exuberant excess of movement may be the main experience and when the freedom is so dominating that detailed phrasing is immaterial, so these times are important for junior-school children also. But in the junior school the work should develop in general more and more towards 'whole-movement' compositions, which are comparable with whole songs and whole poems, and which can be fixed, practised and kept as a repertoire. While the children at the top of the infant school can begin to acquire a repertoire of short, composed sequences, those at the top of the junior school, and at secondary school, should begin to understand the meaning of the art of movement in such composed forms.

This does not mean that some lessons cannot be taken around a movement theme which, though it develops into a satisfactory whole, is not necessarily practised, refined and kept in the repertoire. Such lessons can well be placed among a group of lessons in which a larger idea is developed for individuals, couples, trios, small groups or the whole class.

I do not subscribe to the school of thought which believes that all classes, whatever the age of the children, must master the vocbulary of movement before they can attempt an artistic whole. I believe that a much more positive and involving method of teaching is to work from the whole to the parts. Children will willingly practise all kinds of movement, if they can understand why they are doing it and see how everything fits together. It also makes much more sense educationally for them to achieve an interest in the art itself, and then acquire skills and experiences to improve the art-form. We allow children to paint pictures, sing songs, and act plays, long before they are skilled enough to give a precise performance. The thirst for technique comes from awareness of the weakness of the skills.

Can anyone 'teach' others an art? The answer to this question seems that it is unlikely; but it is possible to help provide opportunities, to provide tools, and to stimulate the right way of looking or feeling or hearing. No one can create to order; a certain time on a timetable does not automatically 'switch on' the children. However, by taking part in an attempt at formulated or 'whole' composition, which captures the shapes and forms and rhythms in our bodies, and yet is bigger and more significant than the 'self' or the individual, we can be 'touched' and made aware, in much the same way as painting or music can 'touch' us. We can work, then, for the recognition of these values in our own efforts, and that of others, and for an aesthetic appreciation.

None of these things constitute art itself, but without them the achievement of an artistic whole is impossible. Although some children will eventually feel the creative drive to pursue one or more of the arts, very few will ever become poets, musicians, dancers, actors, or painters. We cannot control these things as teachers, though, if we are sensitive enough, we can recognise special artistic ability in a child. Most of the children will have moments of creative involvement which are significant to them and to their development, and maybe they will have them when we least expect them. Such experiences of artistic wholeness, fleeting though they may be, are positive and valuable to the individual's development and health, whether he becomes an artist or not.

Is the art of movement of special help to the maladjusted or handicapped child?

Where the normal avenues of teaching have failed, teachers have turned to the arts for help. If hearing speech all the time does not produce speech, the arts may offer a direct way to 'speak' to or 'touch' those children with special difficulties of learning, who are often in special schools. By this approach, they have been helped to relate differently to their problems and handicaps. It would be a pity, though, to allow such recognition of the remedial value of the arts to cloud the issue. Movement is as necessary to the highly intellectually gifted child as to the mongol, to the able-bodied as to the physically handicapped, and to the so-called 'normal' child as to the maladjusted. Because movement touches primary experiences directly, it helps all children to 'keep in contact' with themselves and to develop this essential sense of self. This has nothing to do with being graceful, or gifted in dance or mime, or with being a 'natural mover'. Every baby comes into the world with his own potential range of personality and movement. Nourishing this potential and giving it the opportunity to develop is the aim of movement teaching, both educationally and remedially.

What is the place of the art of movement in the school generally?

In those schools where the art of movement is valued, and where it takes its place beside the other art-subjects, it permeates the outlook and attitudes of both teachers and pupils. In these schools, rituals, dramas, and dances will be performed, just as music is played and pictures and sculptures are made and exhibited. Special celebration concerts related to the school year will be presented, either for the school alone, or for visitors, parents and other schools. These concerts might well include movement as an integral part in a miscellany of poetry, music, movement, and drama, presented by different classes or groups. Sometimes, a whole pageant might be worked out together around a theme which lends itself to this kind of presentation. We tend to think of pageants as 'historical surveys', and this could well be what is needed as a school marks some occasion which calls for celebration—its centenary or the anniversary of its opening, its participation in the town's or district's festivals, and so on. Primitive societies never missed opportunities for celebrations, and these became highlights within the routine which were significant, nourishing and part of the pattern of social and personal development.

Whether the school occasion warrants a large or small-scale

'event' the children and staff who take part will certainly benefit in many ways. As active participants, they make something new. They create a live and vital entity which, again like music, is in one sense ephemeral but in another sense lasting to those who have experienced it. Equally, the observers, who take part by watching, also gain from it.

What kinds of festivals can be celebrated in schools?

First, there are those festivals to celebrate major events in the life of the school, as already suggested. We must take care that on these occasions we do not lose sight of their significance, that is, how we feel, respond and relate to them. This can be understood if we consider the difference between, on the one hand, reading a catalogue of events with dates and places—'And then . . . , and then . . .'—and, on the other hand, following a character or group of people as they lived through those events.

Secondly, throughout the year, there are times we traditionally celebrate, either as individuals (birthdays and holidays) or as a community. Most of these latter 'festivals' have deep roots in our history, and teachers who wish to help children towards both a feeling for history and a feeling for movement, or any other form of art, should read the stories and records relating to them. Children, like adults, can be stimulated to new ideas, or new ways of responding to old ideas, every time they re-encounter a familiar subject whether it is in the arts, in myths, in religion, or in any other sphere of interest. For no one is the same this year—on, say, 'bonfire' night, or at Christmas, or at New Year—as he was last year.

Primitive societies often re-enacted their tribal rituals exactly and precisely, and so kept continuity over the years. Even when they allowed individual or group variations, they kept them within prescribed forms so that the meaning was not lost. The more exactly a society preserved its ritual, over years or centuries, the more stable, or static, that society was. Change, whether growth towards individual development or a breaking-down of a culture, is always accompanied by greater freedom within the ritual, that is, individual or group variations on the prescribed forms. Today, our culture has few of

these totally prescribed or ritualistic art-forms, although there are many lingering attitudes and behavioural patterns. In forms of greeting between people, in eating habits (both the movement pattern and the timing of meals), in the planning of our housing, indeed in all important aspects of life, elements of ritualised cultural patterns emerge. Probably, the Roman Catholic Church has retained the strongest ritualistic sequences, which are both symbolic and dramatic. But other religious groups have introduced or retained their own rituals, which are mostly now very stylised, and often performed solely by the priest, the congregation responding verbally, or with simple actions, at the appropriate moments.

Children in school have very little ritual at the level of symbolic action which can be recognised as belonging to our culture. They do, however, provide a varied and rich diet of ritual play for themselves, even though most adults do not normally see or understand it. The adult has to draw upon his own inner 'knowing', if he is to 'plug in' to the child's world of play and ritual. By this I mean not taking everything at face value but recognising the symbolic meanings and responding to them, either intuitively or from knowledge. However, all parents or adults who are in close contact with young children will be familiar with the almost obsessional need of a child to have a story just right. The story-teller is corrected if he misses a word or phrase. So, too, in their own games, children very often use exact actions, words or sounds at a precise moment in the game, and these games will be repeated over considerable periods of time until the need is satisfied. This kind of strict adherence to form is similar to that of tribal rituals. Children seem to drop out or take part, as they need to, within the groups.

Something of this element of true ritualistic play may be achieved by the children and the teacher working together through movement, and when it happens it is the sign of a positive and fruitful relationship. Sometimes—and this is probably necessary at first—the teacher will take a major part in the composing, particularly if there is a very large group of children. Sometimes, usually at the top of the school when children have had a great deal of experience in movement, they can develop such movement play in groups with only a limited amount of stimulus and guidance from the teacher. But they will need guidance if they are to progress beyond the spontaneous working out of an idea to a developed artistic whole. Mere repetition, though important, is not enough. It is at this point that the sensitivity and knowledge of the teacher is needed.

How can the teacher help development without making inappropriate changes? How can he recognise what the children are trying to formulate when words are not the medium, and they may not be able to put their meaning into words? Certainly a knowledge of the possible vocabulary of movement can help the teacher to understand more fully, as can experience of ways of making phrases, transitions and groupings, though the teacher must always use this knowledge to serve the meaning.

The kinds of questions that he should ask himself, and sometimes ask the children, include the following: What is this phrase, section or scene, trying to say? Is it clearly defined? If not, how can it be made less vague? Is it necessary to cut out a lot of movement? Is there too much vague meandering in space or in rhythm? Do the arms need to be waving about? Would it be clearer if the phrases were shorter? Does the whole build-up lack dynamic stress? Is it flat and too even in timing? Is there a climax? How can the movement be best clarified? Should these movement phrases be repeated to give greater impact and to emphasise the action? Should the size and extension be varied, perhaps growing from a very small to a wide extension in a sequence of phrases? Is this particular meaning best made clear by the whole body in large movements, or by a smaller, more subtle movement of one part? Which part? . . . The questions multiply and should characterise the teacher's attitude in trying to relate to the particular composition, whether it is one made solely by a child, by a group, or by the teacher together with the children.

Seasonal Festivals

A school year starts at harvest time, and progresses through to midsummer.

A Harvest Festival is traditionally held by many schools.

Usually, they link the offering of foods with the school assembly; and sometimes a hosptial, a children's home, an old people's home, or similar centre, will receive the gifts. Harvest offers a good many ideas for country children to produce a harvest ritual or group dance. Town children also can be encouraged to study something of country activities, especially if the work is linked with a country visit, or with a country school. Another obvious link with the theme is an historical study of early man and his progress from a primitive hunter to cultivator of the land.

In such a theme are
    (a) motifs of working actions;
    (b) offering motifs;
    (c) worship motifs;
all ritualised and stylised.

(a) Working actions of the kind used in harvesting are 'whole-body' movements which, enlarged and stylised, symbolise all that man undertakes both in his struggle with nature and in his partnership with her. They symbolise the gathering in of the fruits of the earth, collecting, storing and protecting. If the scope of the theme is enlarged, these actions may symbolise what has gone before, sowing seeds and tending the ground to make the mowing, reaping and harvesting possible. Sequences of such working movements will be developed in phrases of action appropriate to each kind of activity. The rhythms arising from the actions as they are repeated will vary according to the stress or accent, the preparation of the phrase and recovery after it. Through repetition of the movement sequences, a regular rhythm arises; working songs, chants or tunes may be composed, just as the old working songs originally arose from the actual work situation. Continuity and flow help the work along. Transitions occur after groups of phrases which make up whole 'sentences' or 'verses'. Between these groups of phrases, transitions can consist of movements which adapt the body and mind to a new endeavour, direction and focus, or they can be pauses and rests.

When the actions are familiar, the children can be formed into small or large groups, and their pathways around the area in which they are to move can be defined. One group may be fairly stationary, perhaps with the emphasis of their movement going up into space, as, for example, in building a haystack, when the movements will be of pitchforking the hay, lifting it, and throwing it upwards. Another group may be digging, or lifting root-crops, where the main stress will be down into the ground. Another group could be scything with a spreading, horizontal action: this would lead to a travelling motif, covering the ground with long sweeping actions and stepping forward after each action to prepare for the next one. The movements of the different groups both in the starting position and in travelling in the room should be related to each other.

At the end of this scene, a transition would take the children into a new formation for the next scene. If forty children, say, are taking part, the groups can be larger; but also other groups can start at different times, some holding a position, while others are working.

The arrangement of these actions will depend a good deal on the teacher, as the children taking part will be unable to see the whole picture for themselves. The shapes and patterns arising from the movement, including patterns in the air and pathways across the floor, are reminiscent of painting—the hall being the canvas, and the moving characters the colours, lines and groupings of shapes.

(b) Offering to others the first or best fruits of the season (even now when the children are more likely to bring tins of fruit or beans or meat) is a token of offering to God, or the gods. Giving to our neighbour is for the glory of God, working in the fields, in factories, shops or schools, is for the greater glory of God. Early man lived nearer to his gods, and this notion of offering and worship was natural to him and an unquestioned necessity. We have moved a long way from this outlook, especially in the modern world where we are to a large extent divorced from the earth, from the natural and the traditional. Over-competitive attitudes, striving only for material wealth and money, mean that man no longer strives for food in order to live, and there is no longer a close awareness of death, hunger or abundance, all aspects of man's life under the protection of the gods.

Can we, through our rituals of the Harvest Festival,

awaken something of this early closeness to nature? In the dance, the children gather in their arms the corn, fruits and vegetables (or gather them into a large basket) and carry them alone, or in a group, to the place of offering. This carrying to a place, bringing not only the offerings but themselves, is of course symbolic. They leave their fields, homes and working places, and go to a special place. This can be experienced as a kind of processional. Placed down, the offering itself is a giving, not only of external goods, but of oneself. There is no need to carry actual offerings; the body attitudes will show the size, shape, weight and fragility of the imaginary objects.

Such symbolic giving is an integral part of our lives. When we give presents to loved ones, it is always the best, the most beautiful, rather than the unwanted or the left-over that is given. The gift is symbolic of our love. A gift rejected is a rejection of ourselves: a gift offered is an offering of ourselves. The child who does not know how to give is impoverished, whether the giving is of his thoughts, feelings and love, or symbolised in his toys, in flowers specially picked or a present bought from a shop. The more treasured the toy, the greater the gift. And if the treasured thing is given in spontaneous generosity, it will have a different quality from something that is given out of a feeling of guilt or duty. It is, of course, just this inner quality that movement teaching attempts to convey without openly spelling it out to the children.

(c) Worship is an attempt to lift ourselves up into the presence of God, or the gods. It is inspired by awe, the recognition of power which is greater than ours and to which we willingly give praise. Alone, we could not have grown the fruits; the harvest was the result of a partnership of man with the earth. Stylised movement patterns—stable in character, and with the body held symmetrically—contrast with the working actions and the processional journeying. Groupings or massing of children can give impact to the movement, like a choir singing in unison.

This, perhaps, describes the simplest possible way in which the theme could be developed, in three scenes of working, offering and worship (there could also be 'play' scenes between the others). All the scenes are worked out with appropriate motifs to capture the meaning, and placed one after the other in logical sequence. A more complex kind of development of this theme will be described in Part Two.

Photographs can preserve moments in the composition when the body can be seen to capture the expression of the theme. But they are unsatisfactory, just as the description of any art which depends on progression is unsatisfactory if one takes out one moment—for example, a chord in music. It is the movement itself, and the progression from one moment to the next, that is meaningful. A disembodied note is not music; it becomes significant only when notes or silences before and after weave it into the rhythm and shape of the whole.

One way in which this sense of progression can be felt is in the seasons of the year. Tracing seasonal changes can be rewarding both for children and teachers. There are interesting similarities in traditions from widely different geographical areas and cultures, and many ideas can be sparked off by looking into them. Ideas from stories and records should provide the children with a basis for meaningful compositions of their own. Midsummer revels, winter rituals, spring festivals (remnants of which linger in the Church calendar and in our Bank Holidays) all arose out of man's need to make meaning and sense of his life and the seasonal changes he observed.

In spring, the emphasis is on new growth, new birth, new life. The forms and colours of spring, slender, small, clear and simple, are tentative, yet forceful and lively; they suggest individuals meeting others, experimenting with their relationships close to the earth—but aspiring upwards. In contrast, the fruitfulness and richness of autumn, with its rounded shapes, its deep and varied colours and abundance, lead to whole-bodied, vigorous group movement. The winter seasons of cold and icy sparkle, or of gales and rough action, contrast profoundly with the leisurely moods of summer.

Festivals which relate to particular dates, but are not necessarily directly linked with seasonal changes, are celebrated in the Church year. Most of them were originally superimposed on ancient pagan festivals, which tended to survive side by side with them. An interesting mixture of the two traditions can still be discerned. An example is Hallowe'en (the eve of All Saints' Day) which is a fertile source of material in the autumn term: witches, wizards, skeletons, ghosts, bonfires, cats and magic!

The drama of the ritual festival of Christmas is, of course, rarely missed in schools, though many of the forms used have become dull and repetitive, rather than being truly stylised or traditional. The Christmas play need not be a habitually sentimental enactment of the Christmas story. A richness of movement ideas and original compositions in place of a worn-out tableau could give the essential Christmas message a new impact.

At Easter, the enactment of the Resurrection is a Christian tradition. Non-Christian countries often have New-Year Festivals, such as the Chinese rituals.

In England, Guy Fawkes Night has much of the quality of ritual. Its theme stimulates children because of the inevitable excitements of bonfires and explosions! Moreover, the experience has implications which are close to us all. Fire burns and crackles and dies down, fireworks explode and disintegrate; everything collapses, like the empty containers found next day. Hence, to symbolise this ritual, free rhythm, a kind of controlled chaos, is appropriate, accompanied by sounds and noises from objects and percussion instruments.

All these are just some of the ideas that teachers and children can follow up.

Rituals

All aspects of life were symbolised by dance in primitive societies, and these included things like hunting and fishing, as well as birth, marriage, death and war. And today, children, especially junior groups, like to enact the stalking and hunting of wild beasts. The care and skill needed in silent creeping, the attack and kill, the celebration of victory, are aspects which may be included. The exhilaration of being the hunter contrasts with the pain and fear of the hunted. These emotions will echo the inner conflicts of childhood, as well as being a real part of an actual scene.

Ritualised scenes of war and fighting give junior-school

children an opportunity to match themselves against others. Modern 'rituals' of cops-and-robbers and cowboys-and-Indians have the same theme. Any study of the cultures of other people, whether historical or geographical, will lead the children towards ritual ceremonial and dance. Sometimes, an authentic copying of the ritual may be desired and possible, particularly if visitors from, say, Africa or the East visit the school. At other times, the ideas and essence of the ritual can be put into an appropriate form for children here and now. How well such transpositions can succeed and become meaningful experiences for children depends upon the knowledge, sensibility and skill of the teacher.

Stories, myths and legends

Stories full of action offer suitable themes for dramatic or dance compositions. They may be fairy-tales, ballads, ancient or modern myths, stories from the Old and New Testaments, or modern stories. Myths are always concerned with the inner experiences of man, and are, therefore, the stuff of the art of movement; for instance, the pursuit and slaying of dragons, as in the legends of St. George, the Minotaur, and the Gorgon. The heroic action and adventure in Greek mythology is stimulating material. Quests and knightly exploits are common symbolic themes containing allusions to the inner life of man, and will follow on from those dealing with the seasonal festivals, which are concerned with man's need to work with and understand nature.

Modern myths about space exploits and discoveries, and journeys to unknown worlds, are highly popular material for television programmes. But the imagination stretches further than the moon, taking in undiscovered worlds, monsters to be overcome in the shape of other life-forms together with entirely new forces to be faced, and situations to conquer. The essence of such new stories remains the same: quest, discovery and the overcoming and slaying of the enemy within us. The possible identification of the child with the hero or heroine is one of the functions of myths of this kind. It is as if the child's inner struggles are personified outside himself and he has some control over his actions and their outcome.

Magic belongs to our inner life and experiences. The world of children is full of magic, and magical changes of state, such as in being turned to stone or into another creature, or being put to sleep by a spell. The magic can also be reversed and the spell broken by good forces which then triumph over evil, as the fairy prince does in the Sleeping Beauty story. Those teachers who direct all the work of the children towards the external realities (factual information about their surroundings), forgetting the vivid inner realities of fantasy and imagination, fail to provide opportunities for the children to come to terms with their inner conflicts. Emotional development becomes possible when the teacher can give body to the reality of the inner world. The child's ability to differentiate between the two—being, say, the wild beast and still being himself—is a sign of his growing up; babies cannot make such distinctions.

Stories from the Bible are an abundant source of material for movement; they are also, in the true sense of the word, myths. For example, the creation of the world can provide a theme for a whole school for a whole term, the scenes of each phase being developed perhaps by different classes and finally put together at a festival. Experienced older children can make a shorter, but whole, version themselves. (See Part Two for further details of possible development of this theme.) The 'Valley of Dry Bones' has been used as a stimulus for composition. There is a film of junior-school children's movement made in the West Riding of Yorkshire, which includes a simple composition on this theme.[1] Moses, the plagues, the slaves and the flight from the Egyptians provide a major theme for older children. From the New Testament, the Prodigal Son is a favourite story, and many themes from the stories and parables could be studied through movement while the stories are actually being read.

Imaginative and fantasy themes

These themes may occur in stories or poems, or arise from other sources: underwater themes, magic woods, ghosts, witches and wizards and their spell-casting, good and evil spirits, animated clockwork or machines, such as clocks and

[1] *Movement Speaks*, Museum Service, Wakefield.

dolls, fantasy creatures of other worlds, nonsense sounds, the Jabberwocky, the comic adventures of animals and other-world creatures. All these are just a few of the imaginative ideas that children have. Life in another environment (like weightlessness on the moon, the water under the sea, or the 'upsidedownness' of a different planet) can provoke original ideas for compositions. Magic may rest in an everyday object, a glove or a cymbal, for instance (see Part Two for an example of such a composition) or in a sound (voice or percussion) or a word. Power over others is an attractive theme for children, not only the actual possession of power but being spellbound also. The 'spirits' of colours, sounds and objects can come alive and act their stories in movement.

Natural happenings

In *A Guide to Movement Study and Teaching*,[2] a detailed analysis is given of a sequence based on a volcanic eruption. This could be a short sequence, forming a part of a larger, whole composition, such as the Genesis story of the beginning of the world. Magnetism, demonstrating attraction and repulsion, is a vivid movement theme which can concentrate attention between partners. Suction (as in swamps or whirl-pools or the sea in its retreat from the shore) is the kind of force which can be experienced in movement. Animal-like sequences might also be part of a larger composition; cat-like, snake-like and elephant-like creatures can be created.

Growth in all its forms (in rhythm, in size and extension, in intensity, in covering space, and in the related idea of shrinking and dwindling away) occurs frequently, just as crescendo and decrescendo do in music.

Other arts

Ideas for themes in movement can be stimulated by other media. A picture can inspire ideas for whole sequences and compositions, either by the subject matter or by the colour and pattern. Sculptured shapes and forms provoke experiences in our own bodies; the feel and touch of materials can

[2] M. North, *A Guide to Movement Study and Teaching*, Macdonald & Evans 1971. This book also gives further details of movement content and vocabulary.

awaken our sense of movement. Music evokes bodily responses in rhythms and patterns; it can not only stimulate but also form an integral part of the composition. If this is so, the total form and shape is dictated by the music, and must be understood and worked with faithfully. Pieces of music should not be wrenched out of their context; only music suitable for using as a whole should be used.[3]

Character types can provide stimulus for dances such as witches', alchemists', sailors' and clowns' dances. *Commedia dell'arte* characters can be used in new story forms. Usually, the right music will support such compositions and provide a framework for action sequences.

Summary: the movement content

Children in the junior school should be working towards whole compositions, either their own or their teachers' or compositions they have made together. These may be for solos, duos, trios, small groups or for the whole class. The children should gradually gain a repertoire of such compositions which they can master and enjoy, just as they will undoubtedly have a repertoire of songs. Concern must be given in the compositions firstly to the theme, that is, the meaning and the content. In order to make the content clear, the teacher will have to study movement motifs related to:

> *Bodily participation*; which part leads, which takes the weight, what shape it makes, with the stress on economy of action rather than on excessive and meaningless movement.
>
> *Rhythm*; the expressive content and mood, the gentleness or dynamic exuberance, the vitality or leisureliness, the restraint or freedom. These moods result from the qualities of movement which form the rhythms and phrases. Phrases can die away, explode suddenly, increase and decrease, or they can change and transform into new rhythms.
>
> *Spatial patterns*; patterns the body draws in the air as it moves in the space, and the floor patterns which arise from travelling about the room.

[3] M. North and P. Nordoff, *Creative Music for Primary Children*, Macdonald & Evans (in preparation).

Groupings and formations; groups have a body shape and pattern like a single body, but bigger. The group, however, can be split, it can join up again, it can scatter or converge. The group can spread itself and grow large, or huddle closely together and become small.

In all these actions, the children must relate, not only to their own bodies, rhythms and shapes, but to those of others. They learn to respond, initiate, take responsibility and to follow; they learn to be part of a larger whole, as well as to be an individual in isolated movement.

Any composition can occur in silence, where the rhythms are within the action of the body and are not made audible. It can also have percussion or musical accompaniment made for the whole or for part of it, following the movement rhythms. Percussion can be played by the moving children, and voice sounds or words can also form part of the intermingling of rhythms in movement and sound. (See Part Two for examples of this.) Objects can be introduced, such as the magic cymbal, gloves, hats, spears or drums; these are either worn or used as objects passed from one to another. Costume can be worn (head-dresses, sashes and tunics) and they can all be an integral part of the composition.

5 *Practical Movement in the Infant School*

The two main areas of practical movement which are being considered in this book are agilities and the handling of objects.

Agilities, which include activities like climbing and scrambling, involve using the body in an agile and efficient way in response to a variety of different challenges. It must be remembered that not every child has the same attitude and background to such activities. For some, it is frightening to be faced with having to climb on to or over some large, high construction; for others it is immediately a delight and a challenge. The achievement and satisfaction resulting from manoeuvring the body skilfully, or even just adequately, can be invigorating, ˜nd it is equally important whether the child has just managed to jump down two feet or whether he has dared to leap from a towering height.

In handling movable objects (the small apparatus of balls, hoops, bats, quoits, and so on) manual and bodily dexterity is necessary if the objects are to be handled with any kind of skill. The degree of skill found in the infant child varies greatly: some may be extremely dextrous, while others have an almost total inability to catch, throw, hold or aim an object with any kind of efficiency. As with skills which involve agility, the child experiences a great deal of satisfaction and a feeling of well-being when he reaches the stage of handling the objects adroitly.

AGILITIES

Climbing and scrambling, sliding, jumping and landing, crawling, and swinging are some of the opportunities given to the children when we provide climbing frames, ropes, boxes, mats and forms. Children who are developing normally exercise their agilities in crawling, standing, jumping, climbing and so on as soon as they can move about. If one observes young children at play, in a room, or outdoors, there can be no doubt of the attraction of obstacles over which, under which, through which they can climb. In providing such legitimate opportunities for climbing, and extending them to include swinging, a school is doing no more than providing an enlargement of what any normal environment already offers—furniture, trees, fences, walls, stairs, etc.

The teacher plays his part in agility lessons in the normal way of any lesson; his main aim is always to observe, stimulate and respond appropriately to the children at any given time. At the beginning of the infant school, the teacher's actual 'stimulation' may be no more than providing an interesting array of apparatus, well-placed for safety and security, which will give the children the chance to experience a rich variety of agilities. Later, he may set more precise tasks during the lesson which, while limiting the free inventive use of the material, enable a child to formulate and follow a particular action sequence and to invent something new within a more limited field of activity.

No one can give a teacher precise guidance on when he should intervene or set such tasks; child and teacher must respond to each other, each bringing his own sensitivity, intuitions and skills. When a child is ready to progress, the teacher will encourage and challenge him, thus enabling him to work to his own maximum capacity in skill and inventiveness. Sometimes, the class has an overall need for a particular task; it is on these occasions that the challenge will be a general one to which all can respond at their own level.

The kind of challenges can be grouped into those mainly concerned with

    (a)   use of apparatus (getting on, off, over, under, etc.);
    (b)   use of the body (how the weight is taken in balance or movement, body shapes, etc.);
    (c)   the rhythm, timing, quality of movement (accents, phrasing, 'slow motion', etc.).

The apparatus

Most infant schools have some kind of large apparatus,

whether it is easily movable, even by children, or whether it consists of heavier pieces needing to be set up by adults. The kind of apparatus dictates the arrangement of pieces to some extent, partly because much of it has a limited purpose, partly because of the time needed for changing it around. Whatever the actual situation, teachers can easily arrange for changes in the placing of the pieces at fairly regular intervals, say each half term at least and sometimes more frequently. Additional challenges made by employing smaller pieces of equipment can be thought up to supplement the larger pieces; for instance, one can balance canes and hoops on skittles or chairs and provide mats for rolling and tumbling.

First lessons will be concerned with the exploration of the apparatus. From the beginning, teachers should insist upon certain rules for safety and for efficiency. Such rules will not limit the children, but will enable all of them to explore safely, while taking account of the others. The children should not be allowed to push and pull each other; noise should be kept to a minimum of realistic talk when necessary, without shouting and whooping. The crowding of a popular piece of apparatus should be discouraged, since spacing is not necessarily learned automatically by young children. The teacher needs to help by suggestions; for instance, he should make sure there is room to land, and then a place left for others. Such things will often have to be taught, and children who have been to good nursery schools will find no difficulty in such social aspects of the lesson. At the beginning, a teacher might have to point out a particular route along or around a certain piece of apparatus. When this suggestion is no longer necessary, a degree of progress has been made.

Tasks using apparatus

Some pieces of apparatus allow for a variety of uses, some are more restricted. In presenting general tasks such as those listed below, it is often helpful to give the children a chance to move around the room from one piece to another. At other times, grouping them around one 'set' of pieces, so that they have to return each time to the beginning, gives them a stimulus to invent new ways of using the same pieces. Some

examples of tasks are
- (a) moving over, on and off, pieces of apparatus;
- (b) moving under, sometimes without touching the floor;
- (c) moving only on the apparatus, never touching the floor (special arrangements are needed to make this possible);
- (d) moving through the apparatus to avoid touching (this involves squeezing through spaces, twisting and turning carefully, etc. Again, special arrangements will be required here).

Enough time must be given for increasing skill to develop: new tasks on the apparatus can be introduced as the children become confident and at home on it. Feeling confident and comfortable involves managing the body safely, both on the floor and on the apparatus, when jumping, sliding, gripping, swinging, balancing and so on. ·

Tasks which stress the use of the body

These tasks will normally follow the early work on the apparatus, but sometimes a teacher can combine a 'body task' and an 'action task'; for instance, when the children are practising getting on and off the apparatus, they can also try taking their weight on different parts of their body. In fact, given an action task, most children will scramble and roll and balance on different parts of the body quite spontaneously; making this into a special task focuses their attention specifically on it. This should not be done before the child has gained c nfidence and skill in a general sense.

The following are some ways of combining body and action tasks: .
- (a) getting on to the apparatus with feet only touching;
- (b) getting on to th apparatus with hands and feet only;
- (c) getting on to the apparatus with hands first, then knees, etc.;
- (d) getting off the apparatus, hands first or feet first, or rolling from one body part to another;
- (e) balancing on the feet on the apparatus;
- (f) balancing on knees, seat, etc.;

(g) balancing on one foot (later, at the junior stage, stress will be laid on taking weight on hands, with body raised over hands; at the infant level, this is best encouraged at floor level, or on low forms);

(h) hanging on to and clinging to ropes, undersides of apparatus, bars, etc., by hands, or by hands and feet;

(i) changing body shapes either on the apparatus (for example, curling into a ball and then stretching out, as in pulling oneself along a box or form) or when coming off the apparatus (jumping into the air, making a long thin shape, or a wide spread shape, or a turn or twist.)

At all times, the teacher must be aware of the safety factor in giving challenges to children. Most of the challenges are safe when performed at floor level, on mats and often on low forms, or over low sticks. A teacher must make sure that the children are not over-stimulated to attempt dangerous tasks from a height before they can manoeuvre their bodies adequately. It is for this reason I am suggesting that action tasks are mastered first and complicated bodily tasks are not introduced at the wrong time. It is also for this reason that, contrary to many authorities, I do not advocate advanced types of movement training at floor level, and then 'opportunity given for the movement experiences of the earlier (floor level) work to be "applied" in the use of apparatus'. So long as the children are confident and are carefully observed by the teachers, they learn best by being presented with the challenge of the apparatus itself. One of the 'pieces of apparatus' can well be the floor, but to guide the work for all from the floor 'on to the apparatus' is not advisable. Most children work extremely safely within their own capacities and a teacher will quickly be aware of the occasional child who seems to lack an inbuilt sense of his own body's abilities and who will therefore take unreasonable risks.

Tasks related to the timing or quality of movement

Most of these tasks, like the advanced body tasks, will be more appropriate for the junior-school child, though some children at the top of the infant school can begin to manage, for instance,

(a) slow-motion movement in part of their sequence of action;

(b) gentle rolling after a vigorous action, and a spring back into action;

(c) held pauses and balance within a sequence.

It will be noticed that sequences are stressed here. The children need to become aware of the whole sequence of action (the phrase or sentence) from the starting place, into the main action or actions and through to an ending. Such an awareness is the main work which is to be developed in the junior school in the agility lesson. Similarly, although infants can take in spatial ideas, such as travelling backwards or sideways, it is in the junior school that the main stress will be put an awareness of space and of direction.

HANDLING OBJECTS

The lesson with small apparatus can be held equally well in the hall or, in fine weather, in the playground. There should be plenty of pieces of small apparatus, enough for each child to have a ball, hoop, rope, or bat of his own, and skittles and canes to provide targets. Part of the lesson involves the children learning to handle and distribute, collect and store the apparatus, so adequate containers should be supplied. Good arrangement of the apparatus in the hall or playground helps towards a smooth-running lesson. Children should be taught from the beginning to take care of the material they use.

Most children will have played with a ball and some will be quite skilful in handling, throwing, catching and even dribbling it. Other apparatus will be new to them and, over the term's work, they should experience a wide variety of it.

The main way of improving our manual dexterity and our bodily agility in relation to it, is through handling the objects themselves. No amount of isolated practice without the object will really improve our skill at the beginning. Perhaps, at a later stage, there may be momentary value in practising a stroke or an action without the object, but certainly at the infant-school stage, improvement is through practice. So the lesson involves actually handling the ball, hoop, bat, or whatever material is available. Any teacher can think up challenges which will focus the children's attention on a particular skill. To give examples, although free playing with a ball is possible, even young children can respond to challenges such as

(a) make your ball roll in and out of everyone else's; keep your hand (foot) near it to guide it along;

(b) roll your ball slowly, and run to get in front of it and stop it;

(c) roll your ball to a partner a little way away; increase the distance between you as the aim becomes better.

Then by contrast

(d) throw your ball into the air, and catch it or chase it; at first make small throws to make it easier to catch, then let them get higher and higher;

(e) throw a ball to a partner, at first close to and then further away. Try to throw so that he can catch it.

Then combine the two

(f) sometimes throwing the ball, sometimes rolling; play with your partner, near to and getting further away;

(g) bounce your ball; catch it;

(h) bounce your ball many times; keep it going. Bounce it as you go in and out of other people; guide it all the time.

So with hoops, quoits, large balls, small balls, similar tasks can be developed. Each piece of apparatus lends itself to the employment of different skills; small balls can later be handled with one hand instead of two; quoits can be rolled or can be caught by gripping them or by putting the hand through the hole, and so on.

Like this, a whole lesson can be arranged with one piece of apparatus being used in many ways. A different kind of lesson is the one in which many different pieces are used in similar ways. The entirely free 'play with a ball, or a hoop' may be used to advantage as an opening or climax to a lesson.

Work with partners should be practised from the beginning. When only simple skills are involved it presents no problems, but many children will need to play alone for a long time with a bat and ball, hitting it up, bouncing it or balancing it, before attempting the advanced task of receiving a ball from another person. The two-fold problem is of the 'bowling' being aimed precisely, and the need to coordinate eye and hand when hitting a ball coming from someone else. With shuttlecocks or light balls, using the flat hand as a bat is sometimes helpful as a preliminary.

Aiming at a target is a skill which can be started in the infant school; at first the target can be a large area and then gradually it can be made smaller and more difficult to hit as the skill improves.

Group practice can be started at the top of the infant school, but again, this is normally junior-level work. There is really no excuse for large groups to have to work with one piece of apparatus (such as a large ball) when the actual time allowed for handling of the ball by each child is very limited and much time is wasted by waiting for a turn.

Skills which can be developed include:

throwing, aiming, catching, holding, hitting and bouncing. All of these can be practised using different parts of the body (for instance, with right or left hand, with both hands, underarm, overarm) and using space in different ways (throwing high, low or at middle level).

Skills can be developed standing on one spot, or in travelling and dodging. Dodging brings in a whole range of body activities and qualities of movement, such as twisting the body and changing direction quickly to avoid someone else, or jumping into the air to catch a ball and running holding it.

So it can be seen that there are again

(a) action tasks, such as catching or aiming;
(b) bodily agility tasks, such as using right or left hand, foot, or jumping;
(c) quality tasks, with changes of speed and stopping or rushing;
(d) direction tasks, such as dodging sideways, dribbling forwards or kicking backwards.

Combining agility and manipulative skills

This is possible, for instance, when a child rolls a hoop, runs to it and dodges through it, catching it afterwards before it falls; or in skipping, where the rope must be turned so that it synchronizes exactly with the jumping, and so on. Again, these skills are often not achieved until the junior school.

6 Practical Movement in the Junior School

AGILITIES

Junior work on apparatus follows and develops from the infant approach discussed in Chapter 5. It is not intended to give detailed suggestions for lessons here. *Teaching Gymnastics*[1] gives precise suggestions for apparatus, themes and tasks, to which the reader could refer for further details.

All the ideas propounded in Chapter 5 can be developed into more challenging tasks requiring skill. In general, it could be said that progress will be seen

(a) in the more challenging arrangement and height of apparatus;

(b) in the more agile, daring and skilful use of the body, and in greater variety of movement, weight-taking, body shape, balance, etc.;

(c) in the more phrased, differentiated and developed rhythms and patterns of movement;

(d) in the greater variety and skill of direction and spatial awareness;

(e) in the ability to work with other children, both by supporting them and in unison patterns of movement.

The differences in gymnastic agility between children become more and more obvious as they get older. The daring, skilful child of six or seven usually progresses to being a highly-skilled, aware and fluent mover at the upper end of the junior school. The less agile six-year-old may catch up with the gifted mover, but he may also lag further and further behind. Nevertheless, all children should be encour-

[1] E. Mauldon and J. Layson, *Teaching Gymnastics,* Macdonald & Evans, 1965.

aged to develop their skills to their own maximum capacity, in for instance

    (a) climbing;
    (b) swinging;
    (c) sliding;
    (d) balancing;
    (e) clearing heights (flight is one of the junior-school child's big advances over the infant-school child);
    (f) jumping on and off apparatus;

All of these actions, stimulated by the apparatus and the placing of one piece in relation to another, can be performed fairly easily from the age of eight upwards. The teacher's task is to stimulate the children to improve and perfect these skills, and he should begin to demand higher standards of achievement and to encourage repetition and concentration on the demands of each particular task.

In the first place, the teacher should try to arouse awareness of the body in action and in stillness, that is, awareness of body poise and shape and alignment. This poise goes along with the awareness of rhythm and sequence of action, so that although inventiveness is still needed at the exploratory stage, selection of a sequence of actions, followed by repetition and refining of the sequence becomes the main aim. This kind of selection and precision of movement cannot come about until the early stages of exploration and inventiveness have been allowed to create confidence and bodily awareness. Such a demand for facility and skill not only helps the child to deal adequately with his environment, but encourages the greatest possible physical and emotional enjoyment through his own mastery of the skill.

The teacher needs, by this time, to be a good observer of actual skills as well as to have a sound, general awareness of the adequacy of the children. Allowing one or other child to demonstrate can be a way of helping to focus attention through observation. In choosing the children who should show their work, it is often helpful to select two and compare their choice of movement patterns.

First observe whether the task has been fulfilled. If the

task is a bodily one, choose two children who use their bodies differently in the shapes they make and so on. If the task is one of sequence or direction make sure that the chosen children illustrate contrasting ideas in the specific area, both equally good.

Then observe the rhythmic accents or quality of movements, and their appropriateness. It may be that parts of the sequence are very poised and appropriate and that another part could be improved by changing the timing or strength. This can be coached.

So it is possible, with a class with whom the teacher is familiar, to use confident children to encourage the others, not only by praising them but by suggestions for improvement. Needless to say, the choice of the same child or children should be avoided. Every child can do something well, and it is the teacher's task to make sure all have a turn to show achievement.

For the teacher, it is essential to be able to analyse why a movement sequence is not achieving its object. Is it a failure of a bodily kind, or of a spatial pattern, or of a rhythm or sequence?

Older children find it a great challenge to teach their sequence to another child or to a group. It demands from them clarity and precision, and from the others, good observation. Awareness of the rhythm of the movement is encouraged when the sequence has to be performed in exact unison of timing and poise.

In planning the lesson for junior children, the teacher needs to watch their general stages of development and also notice any particular weaknesses. These can form the theme of the lesson, or the continual stress within the lesson. For instance, resilience and bounce may have been poor in one class and this can be emphasised at all stages of the lesson. Another class might be generally lacking in awareness of body shape. The children can work on these points, and the teacher can introduce new ideas, in between using the apparatus. Within the lesson, a good deal of the coaching will be given to an individual child or a small group, and this demands a continued alertness and astute observation from the teacher, based on a wide experience and knowledge of movement.

SMALL APPARATUS AND GAMES

Junior children may be extremely skilful with small apparatus, and many of them are ready for group play, where in the
infant school they had played only with a single partner.
Unfortunately, too many junior schools see 'games' as the
adult team games often played at a professional level, such as
football, cricket, rounders, netball or hockey. These demand
'a degree of physical, intellectual and social maturity which is
utterly at variance with what we see at the primary stage.
Indeed, when one stops to reflect on what the word "game"
means to a child, it is ironical to realise how narrow is the
interpretation placed upon it by adults for the purposes of
education, and how consequently impoverished their imagination in the choice of activities selected for inclusion in the
curriculum under that name.'[2]

Do children need to be taught games techniques?

By the time the children reach the top of the junior school,
they usually want to learn the techniques of the games they
play. Just as in any other subject, the right way to do
something becomes important: it is no longer enough simply
to explore, invent and experiment.

A thirst for precision and accuracy includes also the need
for rules, whether they are invented by the children themselves or taken from major games seen on television or when
visiting the local football ground. Some children will spend
many, many hours practising dribbling, hitting, aiming,
throwing and heading. This is partly because they want to
become more 'adult' and skilful so as to become members of
teams, but partly also for the sheer pleasure of mastery.
Many of the skills of skipping or of throwing and catching
balls (often with three or more balls) on which children
spend a lot of leisure time, have no competitive team game in
view. So a teacher needs to know, by the time this stage is
reached, what is a helpful stance in serving at tennis, or
batting at cricket or rounders, what is the correct (that is, the
most efficient) way to hold and grip the bat or racket, what
sort of a run will help in propelling the ball or quoit.

[2] E. Mauldon and H.B. Redfern, *Games Teaching*, Macdonald & Evans
1969.

Observation of the more skilful children will often give the less knowledgeable teacher some help on this, and there is no reason why children's knowledge gained from parents and older children should not be used for all the class.

It should be recognised that the traditional national games will always hold some sway over certain groups of children who long to copy their heroes. Equally it should be remembered that not all children find their heroes in this area of activity. A good school will cater for all children and, to this end, the results of 'top of the school' competitive team games should not be the only results announced in the school assembly. These competitive games should surely be the club activity of those who wish to spend extra time in this way; and this activity furthermore should be only one of many choices, each valued for itself. All children should be catered for and the gifted and skilled should be given the opportunity to develop, as well as the clumsy and awkward.

Developing from exploration to games techniques

The young junior is beginning to develop his skilful and inventive play with materials from the infant level to the stage of 'games' with others. But such games are closer to his other types of play than to the formal competitive games of adults. Rules, for children of this age, should be few in number and understandable. Left to themselves, children will revise rules, make them, drop them or change them, as the game progresses. Gradually, as they get older, they will be able to keep consistently to set rules, and then they are entering into the next stage as discussed above. Children at the bottom or in the middle of the junior school will play and enjoy 'soccer-like', 'cricket-like', 'throwing' or 'kicking' games. They begin to welcome the added stimulus of objects approaching them from another person or persons and the unexpectedness of the adjustments they have to make in fielding, or gathering, or catching or hitting the ball, quoit, or whatever.

Planning the lesson

Teachers should be able to devise games played in small groups for the young and middle-school juniors, which challenge and extend the various skills of

> throwing, hitting, kicking, aiming;
> catching, gathering (on toe, etc.);
> carrying, or travelling with the objects.

Many easy 'warm up' activities will combine these; for instance, dribbling between partners and passing across to one another while travelling the length of the field or playground; throwing and jumping into the air to catch the ball while off the ground; hitting a ball on to a wall with hand or bat, letting it bounce before hitting it back and so on.

For juniors in the middle and at the top of the school, the main lesson should be a real game, usually in groups of threes, fives or sevens. It is seldom, if ever, reasonable to have full-sized teams. Too few children can take part to any degree if the full number needed for adult teams is used.

The games that develop will bring in one or more skills. They include

(a) the running-type games, passing, or dribbling, where the aim is to get the ball to a certain place without interception from the opposing team, and placing it either by putting it down (rugger type), aiming through goal posts (soccer or hockey type) or shooting through high nets (basketball or netball type);

(b) alternating actions from one team to another (or between individuals or couples) where the area for each team is defined and usually separated by a net or obstacle (tennis and volleyball types);

(c) bat-and-ball games with one team opposing representatives of the other side (cricket, stoolball, rounders type).

Improvised apparatus

Both teachers and children become inventive at using improvised materials for obstacles, targets, 'nets', and so on. Certainly it is unlikely that any school will be able to provide more than a basic supply of formal wickets, nets, or courts. The game can be made interesting and a variety of obstacles can be provided by using all kinds of stands, ropes and skittles. What cannot be improvised are good balls which really have some life and bounce, bats which have quality and spring, rackets which are well strung and efficient. Equipment of this kind needs adequate storage, and children should be encouraged to take care of balls, bats and rackets, not only when using them but when blowing them up, oiling or generally keeping them correctly stacked.

Junior children are active and enthusiastic, and enjoy the kind of games which give them scope for developing their practical skills and playing with others. The sad hanging-about of children on fields or playgrounds, waiting endlessly for their turn, or standing, never touching the ball, is an indictment of the teacher, who shows a lack of awareness of the individual child and a lack of interest or imagination in making interesting opportunities. This waste of time no doubt leads the child to reject games and activities at a later stage.

II Compositions for the Junior and Middle School

7 *Introduction to the Compositions*

Many students and teachers feel that they need guidance in formulating movement compositions. It goes without saying that teachers cannot help children to create compositions in movement, or any other medium, without themselves having experience in the medium and sensitivity to it. Nevertheless, having taken part in other people's compositions does not by itself make the teacher an expert on how it is done.

What is a composition?

Compositions can range from fairly loosely organised sequences of movement, with scope for a great deal of improvisation on each occasion they are performed, to exact and precisely defined gestures, motifs and sequences. A true composition will not be open to great variation each time, just as a piece of music will be essentially the same on each occasion it is played. But those taking part can and should be able to re-create the movement each time the composition is danced or mimed; otherwise it becomes no more than an empty shell of form and pattern and rhythm. If the class genuinely participates in the composition and masters its motifs and meaning in a way that involves their whole bodies, it can be a new experience on every occasion. Whether or not an audience is present makes little difference to this involvement, although an occasional audience to share the experience can often have a stimulting and exhilarating effect on the children. Sometimes the work should be done with performance in mind, but a good composition will always be suitable for sharing with others even when that is not the primary aim.

What, therefore, is a good composition? It must above all else have content and meaning, and it must have been evolved by selecting the most economical and appropriate motifs,

sequences and patterns of movement to express this meaning. As discussed in Part One, this will inevitably involve the
use of movement in its symbolic forms and rhythms, for no
art-form is really art if this symbolic content is not present.

'Creative' is not the same as 'inventive'

When the younger primary-school children have passed
through the purely 'exploratory' stage of movement, the next
step in their progress involves selecting and formulating
patterns, rhythms and forms of movement, either alone or
with others. It does not matter if there are ten different ways
of fulfilling a movement task, so long as one way says clearly
and simply what is required. Inventiveness is not the equiv-
alent of creativeness; it may be helpful to have all kinds of
variations of movement available for use, but, as with poetry,
gaining a large vocabulary will not on its own make creation
possible. It is merely a valuable tool.

The experience of variations and the richness of movement
can, of course, give a wider range to select from, but too often
the teacher of movement is urged to encourage the children
to greater inventiveness by saying 'How many ways can
you . . .' at the expense of using a limited vocabulary with
meaning and significance. The two should go hand in hand.

The more advanced a group is, the greater the degree of
precision and formulation which is possible. Although age
itself is not the only criterion, one would expect a group of,
say, seven-year-olds to have a looser framework and a higher
degree of spontaneous and improvised movement within a
composition than adults who are attempting to master a
composition at its highest level. At that level, even 'chaos'
becomes precisely organised chaos, an effect to be deliberately
achieved.

The ideas for compositions which are included in this book
therefore range from the fairly free to the exact and precise. It
will be found, of course, that even the freer style becomes more
fixed and definite through repetition and practice. Within even
the least precise compositions, definite fixing of 'key' places
and times and happenings are crucial, otherwise the whole
becomes merely a meandering incoherence.

Sometimes, music will fix the vital moments; sometimes it

will be something within the group—a sound, a rhythm or a particular positioning in space. Either way, those taking part must know these key places and adapt to them.

Many compositions which later become exactly fixed in sequence and timing, start as improvised, experimental ideas. Other compositions are more strictly structured and formed from the beginning, either in musical structures, or in body motifs, or in rhythm, or in all of these together.

Choice of appropriate themes

The choice of theme depends not only on the age and development of the children, but on their interests and absorptions at any given time. The teacher who needs an exact programme worked out for the year is probably insecure and apprehensive himself. Such a programme would prevent him from taking up ideas and interests as they arose. However, this is preferable, no doubt, to the teacher who plans nothing in the hope that something will arise from the children. Teaching involves a subtle mixture of pre-planning and the ability to respond to happenings spontaneously. The more experienced teacher can be expected to change his ideas to adapt to new interests, but he also has a richer background of material to draw upon for this. Students and young teachers should plan both lessons and compositions, but still be prepared to adapt them and change their plans if a better idea emerges during the classes.

Themes can arise from any activity, study or interest of the teacher or of the children; from a poem or story; a picture or model; a historical epic or event; music or sounds or words; patterns and colours in nature; natural forces and actions; chemical actions and reactions; dreams or fantasies; materials or toys; current events, such as wars or disasters, explorations and space flights. These are a few of the many possible examples.

The first group of suggestions is for children working in twos, or in two small groups. They are mostly ideas arising out of a theme which could be developed by children for a series of lessons. Within the general structure of the theme and its development, each couple will compose its own sequences, and older children will manage to develop such a sequence into a composed form.

8   Duo Compositions

THEME: MAGNETISM

This is a good movement theme to start off a group. It might have arisen from classroom work, or, if not, a magnet should be brought in so that the children can discuss it and play with it before the movement lesson in the hall.

Movement vocabulary

This theme involves the following things in this order of importance:

(a) relationships between partners, through

(b) parts of their bodies leading and following each other;

(c) 'spatial awareness' (that is, being aware of the levels at which parts of the body move, and the patterns they make);

(d) qualities of freedom and 'boundness' (being confined within a limited space) and of explosion and breaking away.

Here is one example of how such a lesson might be presented.

Introduction

First of all this needs to stress the child's own movement as he balances on different parts of his body, transfers his weight, or stops, poised. It is a matter of 'phrased action'. The emphasis is mainly on his physical agility in taking his weight on his hands, or on his hands and feet, in rolling from seat to side to knees, rolling forwards or backwards, and so on. But as the child achieves an awareness of changing balance and held pauses, this will transform the practice from something purely physical to something 'whole bodied', in that he will have a real inner sense of the way his body is moving.

This part of the lesson can be followed by the children working with partners, developing phrases of movement that involve spinning together while turning slowly, keeping their weight balanced; turning slowly, with hands and other parts of body close but not touching or gripping (this means that the child must move as an individual, controlling his own weight but at the same time adapting to the movements of his partner). Phrases using this idea of moving exactly together could follow, rising and sinking for instance, or travelling a few paces from the spot.

This section introduces the ideas of relationship and working together.

The main part of the lesson

Movement experiences   The teacher introduces the theme, showing the kinds of movement involved. For instance, he can demonstrate with two hands how one leads and the other has to follow because of the strong magnetic attraction. Children in a sitting position could do this themselves, watching their hands carefully. The hands do not need to touch (one can imagine the force working across the space between them) and keeping them all the time a few inches apart helps to develop acute observation and concentration.

Phrase 1   Everyone starts with a partner, the first one having the magnetic power, the second having to follow wherever the other leads. Number one chooses one hand and approaches his partner with that hand, a magnetised hand, presenting the most important part to him. Preferably, he should choose the inside, sensitive hand surface. This hand approaches that of the partner and, as a pin jumps to the magnet when the force is felt, there is a change at that moment in Number Two's body alertness and even in his position. This is followed by a slight pause.

Phrase 2   The magnet partner leads, making the other follow, high, medium, low, making him twist and turn and even somersault to keep the 'contact' distance and to follow the leading hand. The leader must take care of his partner and make sure, while challenging him, that his hand moves with appropriate timing and that its position is always clearly defined.

This part can develop into a series of phrases. They can be freely improvised on each occassion or, for a more composed form, certain rhythms and certain patterns in space can be selected and repeated. By making a selection and repeating it, the children can anticipate the action, the rhythms can be clearer, and the patterning precise. This is the beginning of composition.

The selection of phrases can include such things as

(a) travelling near the floor and rising high;

(b) travelling and turning as the phrase develops;

(c) staying near the floor, but varying the action in front of and behind the body (which means twisting and turning);

(d) rising and jumping;

(e) swooping from low level to high and back to low, on different parts of the body, either standing on one spot or moving around;

(f) staying on the spot but moving near to and far away from the body, as well as using varied levels and patterns round the body.

These or similar tasks can be presented by the teacher, usually one at a time, when the children have first explored the theme of magnetism rather more freely.

Phrase 3 The break-away. The partner who follows begins to tire of this slavery, and animates his hand and whole body to pull away from the magnet. The children should practise this phrase of movement individually, starting with a weak pull but getting stronger and stronger until the pull is very hard, and at last explodes, breaking away to freedom. Then they should return to their partners to practise this section separately.

Phrase 4 This last phrase shows what happens to the magnet and to the partner, and it can be worked out to solve both these problems. The magnet might collapse on to the floor, all its power spent, or it might draw back into itself, guarding its hand, into a poised position, ready to approach again. The free partner might whirl and turn and roll or jump away, emphasising the free flow of this movement, contrasted with the bound and limited flow of the preceding phrases.

Throughout the presentation of the work it is a good idea to start with the whole sequence, roughly indicating phrases and action and endings. Then, when the children see what the whole is like, they can return to each phrase in succession, sometimes practising alone and then with partners, though usually with the partner breaking away for a practice alone and returning again. As each part of the sequence is selected and fixed, it can be related to the other phrases, so that the whole sequence is kept in mind. More than one lesson can be devoted to this kind of work in couples, some of the phrases being left freer and improvised in the first lesson but fixed in the second. Even the improvised work should be clearly phrased.

If the work is phrased straight away, either by an outer sound, or by the suggestion of moving and 'freezing' in a position, the children are encouraged towards formulation. The actual series of phrases used can be presented so as to make contrasting rhythms and patterns and lengths, and if these are given for the whole class, the teacher must be very exact in repetition. Voice or percussion can be used.

According to the age and experience of the children and the length of lesson, such a sequence will take from one to three or four lessons to achieve.

The end of the lesson

This should be a good proportion of the time, not just the last two or three rushed minutes. Whatever the level of their achievement, the children should have a chance to go through the sequence at least once with guidance, and at least twice on their own, taking the responsibility for listening to the sound, without the teacher's interruptions or help. Beginning positions, clear phrasing, held pauses, action content and ending positions can be coached between the repetitions.

RELATIONSHIPS BETWEEN PARTNERS

Before giving further examples of sequences which could be stimulating ideas for a class, let us look at the relationships which are possible between twos. The theme of magnetism is an example of one partner dominating the other, not in fighting, but in leading and following.

Leading and following

Although many beginner students feel more secure with a 'practical' theme, like magnetism, the same idea can be developed without such imagery. The ability to lead, and to follow, are both human capacities which can be encouraged. Leadership demands self-mastery, clarity of movement and decision, and care for the partner. In the movement, this means making clear spatial patterns, timing them so that the partner can follow, producing clear rhythms and accents within the phrases, and placing the body so as to project the desired 'message'. If the leading is done by touch, instead of depending upon the follower's observation, subtle variations in degrees of sensitive and firm movement are required. The simplest task is leading by one hand touching lightly on a partner's hand. A different experience is gained if the follower has the confidence to close his eyes and to respond only to the touch—genuinely to 'put himself into the hands of another'. Such gentle but firm guidance can be developed by contact through other ways of touching, for example turning a partner by placing the hand around his waist, on a shoulder, under the elbow, and so on, which is the kind of leading necessary in ballroom dancing.

The ability to follow demands willingness to be led, together with clear observation and/or response to touch. These are all dependent upon trust in another person and in oneself. The insecure child can neither lead nor follow well, but can gain confidence in such play situations.

Other leading-and-following themes can be thought out. A leader might be at a distance, giving his commands through gestures and body action, like the conductor of an orchestra. He can indicate not only the positions, floor patterns and travelling motifs, but the qualities within the phrases, for instance the bounciness, the light gliding, the vigorous stamping, the swooping and stopping, the apprehensive passing, to name a few. Just as the conductor of a choir or orchestra 'dances' with his whole body, with his face, his trunk and legs, as well as his arms and hands, so it is necessary for this movement leader to move throughout his body and not only to give isolated hand gestures.

On another occasion, a leader can actually move ahead,

relying on the follower to go along with his phrases of movement and rhythms, like a leader in battle, or the leader of a mountain-climbing team, or an explorer in the jungle. At first the child who is following will simply copy the route and the general action phrase, but a more subtle development of motifs can grow out of this idea, so that the pair move in unison or in phrases of movement one after the other. This involves selection and therefore the beginnings of composition.

The 'lead' can also come from behind, like a wind blowing relentlessly, or a person rounding up a crowd, or a partner. A response to such a force might lead to whirling, turning, flying, falling, rolling, or, if the quality is different, to a gradual crumbling, shifting of position, or tough resistance.

All these ideas of influencing by leadership can be performed with partners or groups. The floor patterns will change if a group is used, as more space is needed for manoeuvring; different rhythms will also emerge as more time is needed; different motifs are possible, with groupings arising from the children splitting up, meeting, surrounding others, dispersing and so on.

Matching of power: conflict

Such a situation can lead to

    (a) fighting as equals, enacting battles, comic fights, or the rivalry of a game;

    (b) overpowering and subduing, as ordinary human beings or with magical powers like those of snake-charmers, magicians, witches;

    (c) avoiding and pursuing, as humans or animals;

    (d) catching and escaping.

The situation of conflict suggested in example (a) arose in the magnet theme when the partner tried to resist the influence of the magnet, began to pull away, and finally broke away to freedom. This whole aspect of the matching of power and the ensuing conflict involves counter-movement, in direction, in strength and in timing. Action and reaction, situation and response, are fundamental. The difference between reacting and responding lies in the instinctive nature of the one, and the more whole 'human' nature of the other.

Response is not necessarily predictable, whereas reaction almost certainly is. Perhaps there is a greater degree of choice for the person who can respond, and who is usually more conscious and aware, than for the person who reacts instinctively, always within his own pattern of behaviour.

(a) Fighting as equals involves blow and counter-blow, each partner trying to get the better of the other. This can be a serious enactment of a battle scene, or it can be a comic fight, or even, for instance, a matching of skill in a mimed ball game. The positons of the body will be in counter-tensions: one partner may be attacking forward, and extended, the other withdrawing and covering, only to gather his strength to counter-attack. This counter-attack may involve an upward preparation for a crash downwards, a sideways swing for an attack to the opposite side, or a crouching for an upper thrust. Meanwhile the original attacker goes on the defensive, by withdrawing, or crouching, or turning away, or leaping into the air, or tumbling over. Timing is crucial. Total equality of strength applied simultaneously leads to an evenness, a forceful pressure and holding, with perhaps only a slightly uneven movement, until the clinch (whether a literal holding or not) is broken.

(b) Overpowering and subduing can be the result of the conflict, after matching strength, or it can be a situation inherent in the relationship, as in the magic power over a victim; the overlord over a slave; the snake-charmer over the snake. The movement motifs here will involve, as the words suggest, 'over' movement, that is, one partner towering, superior, on top, with the other partner in counter-positions, such as grovelling, crouching, cowering below. How the subtle distinctions of quality are made will indicate the inner attitudes of the two; for instance, the slave, beaten and cowering, can still indicate defiance with his hand and eyes, or he may be acquiescing; the victim can struggle against the power of magic, and so repeat the motif, or he can change and acquiesce. 'Even a worm will turn' expresses the change in attitude from giving in to opposition, a change of position and therefore attitude.

(c) Avoiding and pursuing brings all the hunting stories,

rituals and searches to mind. The hunted animal, or man, can be terrified and fleeting; can be wily and crafty; can be arrogant and strong. The motifs are of hiding and revealing, chasing, surrounding, escaping, with rhythmical and qualitative phrases suited to the mood; for example, 'terrified fleeing' will be either over-free, dispersed, 'mindless', aimless, agitated, breathless and formless running, falling, jumping, whirling; or rigid, vibrating, narrow, tight, scurrying, 'petrified', stopping and starting. 'Wily craftiness' will be controlled, economical, subtle, careful, agile, both lively and sustained, precise in timing. 'Arrogant strength' will be typified in an upright body (even when near the ground), contained, 'looking down the nose', forceful and efficient in action. Sometimes the roles become reversed, and the hunter is pursued. This can happen when the initiative is lost, perhaps owing to the inefficiency of the hunter, his lack of concentration, or his lack of skill, strength or courage. In group compositions, overwhelming numbers, moving in unison, are often used to symbolise the power of the pursuer and the inevitability of the outcome. Only the truly wily on these occasions can 'turn the tables'. A more evenly matched contest of power, where forces are equal, whether between animal and man, or between either animals or men, would belong to section (a).

(d) Catching and escaping are the hazards of the conflict and are motifs which appear throughout most compositions of this nature. The actual catching is often preceded by many 'near misses', times when the victim is captured but not securely enough to hold him; either his courage, or his strength, or his wiliness, or his desperation give him power to escape, to break through the barriers to freedom, or partial freedom. Exhaustion often leads to capture in the end and this would be shown in a general slowing down of the movement phrase, and also in reactions to new situations. Situations involving groups lend themselves to a greater variety of ways of catching and of escaping from a trap or formation. A group can also present menacing power more easily than an individual through movement in unison, just as a group of singers, drummers or violinists add sheer weight to a musical statement.

Cooperation: working together

This can be seen in

(a) unison phrases of movement, when the couple are side by side or one behind the other;

(b) mirroring, when the couple face each other, or move in counter, complementary directions, e.g. side to side, or as in sawing together;

(c) echoing a movement, or continuing a movement to emphasise it through successive phrasing, with or without overlap;

(d) different positions and actions combining to make a whole action. For example, one partner can hold up an imaginary object while the other supports it from underneath; or one partner continues the pattern of the shape or rhythm set by the other; or the two together make a larger body shape.

Both (a) and (b) are matters of where the two partners are placed in relation to each other, as in each case the movement is in unison, and usually equal, that is, the same movement is performed by both at the same time. This emphasises the motif. A ritual gesture and motif of, say, adoration, becomes intensified if more than one body performs it. In terms of sound, mass choirs, mass bands, mass drumming have the same meaning. A common motif for a group gives a feeling of belonging to each member; each is one unit of a great whole. Two people synchronising their movement symbolise being together. Subtle variations of being together, but with slight personal differences, indicate that the two are individuals, cooperating.

In (c), echoing, the initiating movement phrase is picked up and copied. Usually the echo, or shadow, is a slighter, sometimes distorted, image of the original. If it takes independent life, the idea belongs to the previous section (matching of power) or to the following section. Successive movement phrases may, like the echo, start after a pause, or they may start during the previous phrase and so overlap it. A different rhythmical sequence arises as each phrase (initiating phrase and echo) starts with its own accent. The total effect is like two instruments playing together, and indeed the moving couple can well follow a musical or percussion lead.

The idea of combining to form a joint shape or action (d) is an obvious one. If what is being stressed is the shape of the phrase and its position in space, the second mover can well take the movement further along its pathway, that is the two partners move sucessively. The same thing can be done with the rhythm of the phrase, the two partners picking it up successively. Alternatively the second partner can support the rhythm exactly, or can support it but be different, with the main beat and pulse sustained, but different accents stressed. Cooperative movement can also be used to create a larger body shape, for example an eight-legged monster, or a twisted structure.

Two individuals with their own characteristics

A couple can build sequences involving
    (a) meeting and parting and passing;
    (b) conversation;
    (c) cooperation.

Meetings and partings are part of the human condition. Relationships arise through the way of meeting, as well as the ways of being together as seen in the previous sections. In movement sequences and compositions the meetings will take place in space; at the simplest level, two people start a long way apart and walk, run, jump, roll towards each other. Contact is made, for example, by holding hands, touching finger tips or linking arms. The meeting is emphasised when motifs of staying together follow it, perhaps in turning together, whirling, jumping, or travelling to a new place. The mood or quality is different according to the style of meeting; it can be done reluctantly and cautiously, enthusiastically (with lively energy), sensitively (with fine touch) and so on. The phrase of movement which makes up the approach and meeting can be subtly varied or straightforwardly simple: for instance, a phrase starting with seeing the person a long way off creates an immediate response of free lively surging forward, slowing down and becoming cautious as the two get nearer.

Many more subtle meetings occur in more advanced compositions, as when the couple see each other at a distance, perhaps making a small gesture of recognition, and the meeting then develops into a full motif. The meeting may not involve actual physical contact, but movement rhythms and patterns inter-relate to keep the idea of it alive.

The moment of meeting, the moment of the touch, whether physical or not, is the crucial highlight. Similarly, with parting, the moment of parting is the climax—the release of hands, the breaking of the eye-contact. Such leaving or parting can be lingering or sudden, but there is a moment when the touch is lost. This can be accented in movement sequences to emphasise its significance. 'Passing-by' is a kind of non-meeting, a sliding past, an avoidance. The kind of passing-by in which one partner does not notice the other is a passive thing; it is a 'non-relationship'. The passing-by in which one partner does notice the other and is aware, maybe even regretful, is active and conscious. Movement motifs can be developed which emphasise the attitude of the passers-by, for example, scornful, overpowering, cringing, reluctant, coy, hesitant.

Conversation (b) involves moving in alternating phrases, as a spoken conversation implies one listening to the other and then responding. At the beginning it is helpful for one partner to hold a position, watching the moving partner and only starting his phrase when the first one stops still. Later, a more subtle accompanying movement can be introduced, as when the watcher or 'listener' makes small, responsive movements during the pause. In this way, a listener may nod, smile, say 'yes' and make other acknowledgements in a spoken conversation. If the two are moving and playing percussion at this time, the sound play also becomes significant.

The cooperation (c) of two different individuals can be seen when they mutually support each other, for instance by taking each other's weight. Some examples are a father swinging a child into the air and catching him; one person using another as a kind of climbing frame; two people leaning on each other for support, either back to back or sideways. Caricatures of types such as clowns, sailors, policemen and footballers can all produce their own motifs and sequences of mutual dependence.

Developing motifs and sequences from a gesture
Meeting, being together in unison or conflict or cooperation, and then parting again—these are the actions possible for two individuals or groups. They provide the material for compositions based on relationships. As has been outlined in this chapter, there are many variations on these simple ideas, both in what happens and in how it happens. In a movement composition, one or more of these motifs will form the central vocabulary for the theme. The more dramatic theme will develop in sequences. The lyrical will develop through a repetitive motif in what might be called a more 'circular' or musical form, as distinct from the dramatic straight line. In any theme, whether dramatic or lyrical, ritualistic or formal, it is likely that many of these motifs will appear. The larger the group, the fewer the actual motifs likely to be involved. In working in twos, a large number of motifs, with variations, will be necessary to evolve a complete composition.

Variations in the gestures and motifs of each individual occur in

(a) body placement: that is, how different parts of the body become involved in the movement, in supporting the gestures, in which part leads and so on;

(b) size: growing or shrinking in size can lead from one motif to the next, and phrases of movement may vary in length and intensity parallel with this variation;

(c) placement in the space around the body: what happens near the floor can be lifted higher or sink lower; shapes and patterns of gestures can occur in different directions, as well as in different zones around the body;

(d) quality: intensity can increase or decrease; timing can accelerate or decelerate, can become agitated or calm; restraint can ease, and become freer and more open, or freedom can become inhibited; attention can become more focussed and directed, or more flexible and less directed.

Variation of the motif between two people (that is, variations in the relationship) can occur similarly

(a) in body parts, body shapes, body parts touching, between the two;

(b) in extension;

(c) spatially in directions, zones, and shapes;

(d) in quality, as the phrases are built between the two, echoing, substituting, completing a phrase and so on.

FURTHER EXAMPLES OF THEMES FOR DUOS

Having considered duo relationships in general, let us now look at some other lessons and compositions suitable for junior children working in twos.

Slow motion conflicts appeal to older children and demand enormous control and skill, both in mastery of the quality of sustainment and flow, and in precise and accurate timing between the two. Two ideas are given here: a mimed ball game and a comic fight.

The ball game

Although this sequence suggests the game of tennis, any of the ball games could be used and they would stress different mimed actions according to whether the motifs were mainly concerned with the use of the feet (as in soccer), the handling of a ball (as in rugger, netball, basketball) or the use of racket and ball (as in this example).

It is obvious that such a theme can only be used when the children are familiar with handling the actual materials: the mimed play should not be concerned with skill in that field but rather with the element of conflict, opposition and relationship between the two people. Exaggeration of both the action and the personal reaction and response is often the outcome. The despair, the elation, the intensity of concentration, colour the quality of the action and permeate the bodily expression. When these elements are no longer merely expressed, but formulated into motifs and sequences in rhythm and form, they become the material for composition.

Introduction Every teacher will find his own way of introducing the material of the theme. One possibility is to suggest to each child that he mimes the action of holding a racket and bounces a ball with it, on the floor, in the air, leaping to hit the ball or scooping it up near the ground. The idea here is to try to show exactly where the ball is at any given moment, to follow the ball by looking keenly, and to prepare the body to receive it or hit it again. How the hit is made dictates the action of the ball, whether it flies long and high, bounces sharply, or whatever. It is a simple transition to play between partners. The phrasing of action is dictated by the way the partner responds, and how the ball has to be followed, chased, or jumped for, in order to return it to the partner. A degree of skill and flair can be shown, probably far beyond that which is possible in actually playing the game. (Note here that this is similar to many circus themes, such as juggler sequences, where the 'handling' of material is important.)

Developing the sequence The structure of such a sequence is inherent in the idea; partners alternate actions, with a preparatory movement phrase before the action and a recovery phrase after the return. Timing becomes crucial to the alternating sequences, the preparation happening during the partner's action and the flight of the ball. Exploratory work is not free and vague in this situation, for the limitation of spacing, timing and action is clearly dictated by what the partner does, and by the interaction between the two. The exploratory part lies in choosing how to return the ball, in the body preparation, the quality of effort of the phrase used, and the 'mood' which accompanies this action. For instance, the player can strain to reach the ball, and perhaps afterwards fall over; or he can return it with easy nonchalance, or with the elation of a smooth action sequence.

After the exploratory time, it can be suggested that the children select three action sequences (or more if the class is experienced) with a return from the partner. The teacher can help by limiting this choice at first to one service and its return, and repeating the action pattern of this many times, to decide the body action, the rhythmical phrasing, the spatial placement, and the follow-through (or recovery phrase) of each partner. At this point, suggestions for exaggerating the size of action (leaping, rolling over in recovery, and so on) can be introduced, or they can be recalled if they were introduced earlier in the session. The sequence will develop from the ending positions of the first phrase, and a second motif can be added, preferably a different action with different preparation and recovery. The difference might be in extension (small restrained movements near the body, contrasted with large expansive ones), or changes in level or in height, in force or direction can all enrich the action sequence. It can help if the teacher coaches one of these only, as this concentrates awareness. If the whole sequence is to be complete in three phrases, including the hit and its return, the third phrase will end with each partner, in an appropriate position, one of them presumably having defeated the other. Each one must also show the appropriate quality in the final action.

Such a sequence is a kind of skeleton for a real composition based on this matching of skill and prowess; it can develop into the statement of a relationship, according to the choice of character each child makes. This might be left to the class. It can also be an exercise in mastering a particular kind of relationship, with the teacher setting the type: for instance, one is tall, arrogant, efficient and skilful, the other anxious, earnest, scurrying and humiliated. The ending can be an obvious defeat of the weaker, or a twist of fate can lead to the defeat of the arrogant ones—a typical Chaplin type of sequence, where the 'little' man often overcomes impossible odds by innocence or guile.

The ending At the end of the session, whatever the level of the composition, a chosen and developed sequence should be repeated. Younger children may not be able to compose or remember more than the three basic phrases. Older children can well develop the sequence fully, with repetitions, variations, comedy actions and precise endings. The whole thing can be developed at normal speed, or it can be slow motion. In the latter case, the whole sequence might be completed before the slow motion is introduced, or it might be part of the exploratory play at the beginning.

A comic fight

The idea of a fight is one of the easiest for children to recognise and involve themselves in. Older boys will enact fighting scenes in many different ways, miming the use of fists, swords, bows and arrows, or hurling objects, and the

fight may become part of a whole drama, such as a battle scene or something in the style of *West Side Story*. To avoid muddle ('expression' without form) the sequences need organisation and selection, that is, they need composing.

Preliminary practice In the preliminary practice, each member of the class will act as if he were attacking a particular part of an opponent's body. At first, this attack can be mimed without an opponent, in a kind of shadow boxing, until the idea of holding a position after the hit is achieved. The whole class, in fact, can make as if attacking the teacher from a distance! If the area to be attacked is defined, as when everyone attacks the head, for instance, or everyone attacks the legs, or pierces to one side, then the teacher can make appropriate responses with his body. Here the whole class can respond as if being attacked by the teacher. The class can then be left to work out their own defensive actions. The teacher might say, for example, 'I shall now attack your head. Imagine that I'm going to hit your head and dodge at the moment when you would be actually hit if you did not move.' This will stimulate quick, lively stepping aside, twisting of the body out of range, or backing away. The teacher can give a different stimulus if he suggests that the class does not avoid the blow but parries it on an upraised arm, or with an imaginary sword which will push the attacking sword away. Or again, the defender can be too slow to dodge, and be hit on the head and thrown to the ground.

Before couples are put together to play this hit-and-response action, a good deal of practice is necessary to be sure that the children have the idea of a phrase of action, that is a sequence of preparation, attack and the momentary holding of the position of attack. Children are usually able to enter into the spirit of a game of this sort without starting a literal fight: if the teacher is not sure of this with his own class, then he should not choose a theme of this type.

The interesting part lies in the variety of response to an attack, and the variety of the attack itself. At first, the children may be able to explore freely and to respond according to the particular attack made by the opponent. Given imaginary objects, such as a sword, a stone or a club, they will make appropriate responses to the action. The action should alternate between the partners: first one approaches, attacks and holds the position, and the second one responds (end of first phrase); the second one now becomes the attacker and makes a new attack from the position he took up when he fell or retreated or held off the attack. The first attacker now needs to defend himself (second phrase). For the third phrase, it could be left to the children to devise a simple ending: one may defeat the other in triumph, or the two may face each other with their strengths equally matched so that the struggle is never resolved. Such a simple sequence of phrases would perhaps be sufficient material for the first lesson, provided the teacher uses his knowledge of movement to encourage the children to vary their action and reaction. Different parts of the body may make the attack and different parts of the body may defend, different speeds may be used, and it is here that the slow motion effect can bring a comic element to the whole sequence. The delayed reaction, the delayed attack, the gradual clutching of an injured part instead of the immediate folding up, are ways of producing a comic effect. Slow motion also allows the children to use their agility and their ability to balance, and control their bodies in slow motion rolls, twists and leaps, as well as using sounds and facial expressions.

Development   To develop this idea into a real composition requires a kind of story. What is to be the starting position, and the opening situation? Is one partner quietly playing alone and then the other enters and interferes with the game, which makes them begin fighting? Do both partners enter 'looking for a fight', so that both appear from a distance and, when they see each other, stop? (This is a similar situation to that in *West Side Story* when gang members are on the lookout for an opponent.) Situations in which a fight might occur can be devised by the children, or presented to the whole class at once by the teacher.

The fight then develops and, if the children are less experienced, it is useful for the teacher to control the situation by giving clear, phrased action sequences. For instance, phrase one can be slow, gathering strength for a very pressing kind of hit; phrase two a jabbing, immediate response; phrase three leading into a tortuous, pressing, twisting action; phrase four a series of jabs with the rhythm changing throughout. Whatever the number of phrases decided upon, they must finish with a clearly developed section which defines the final situation and the final positions of those taking part.

If the children themselves are left to devise their own sequences without an outside rhythm, it is useful to stop them in the middle of their compositions and encourage them to make a sound accompaniment while half-miming the action, in order to make them aware of what rhythm they are using. Without this awareness, it will be much more difficult for them to repeat exactly the sequence composed.

Working with children in this way is easy when there is one couple only. It is much more difficult when a whole battle scene is being composed, even if the work is mostly being done in couples throughout the major part of the scene.

For instance, two opposing armies can march in. The battle scene itself will be a fight of couples and, according to the story, it could end with the stragglers from the two armies collecting together an opposite sides or with one army being totally victorious. If more than one couple is taking part, there is the opportunity for cross-timing the actions, so that there is not just a simple repetition of phrase, and this creates a very exciting, rhythmical build-up throughout the group. It will be irregular but not uncontrolled; each couple knows exactly its own timing, its own sequence and its own ending, but the confusion of a battle scene can well be portrayed by this counter-positioning and counter-action.

The first phrase for each couple will be differently placed in space; for instance, some children will hit high, some low, some will leap into the air to avoid, some will roll on the ground, some will travel. The first rhythmical phrasing will be different, the action of one couple will be very sudden, another very sustained, another delayed in action, so that the actual impact of each attack is differently timed. Yet, with each couple, the sequence continues and achieves a precise timing.

Now for all this to become a comic fight, instead of a

more realistic dramatic action, contrasts and unexpected reactions will be needed. Children are extremely gifted in devising comic situations: for instance, an exaggerated preparation with a tiny little prod for the attack; unexpected uses of different and unlikely parts of the body; unexpected rhythmical action that is inappropriate to the attacking theme; and, as previously suggested, slow-motion action which gives ritualistic, comic or 'unreal' effect; the look of triumph on the face slowly dissolving into exaggerated despair; the total collapse into a weak position of a body previously held in triumph; the ineffectual thrusting of a weak drumming action of the hands, and so on. All of these will be found to give a comic aspect to the situation.

In general, a sequence of this kind can be either one small section of a large composition, where a fight scene is part of the whole drama, or it can be a lesson or series of lessons in their own right, depicting this particular kind of action.

9 Compositions for Young Juniors

MAGIC CYMBALS

Magic resides in the instruments, and whoever holds them can exercise power over his victims through magic phrases of sound. This magical power can change people, either in their shape and form or in the way they behave as the gods could change humans in Greek mythology[1] or as Bottom is changed in *A Midsummer Night's Dream.*

The drama arises from the conflict between the evil ones—the witches, gnomes, spirits, and so on—and the children. The evil ones could also be comic and, in another composition, the magical changes could be brought about not by musical instruments but by some other object such as a piece of clothing.

The translation of these ideas into movement happenings can take many different forms. One example would be to formulate the story into three scenes, or sections:

(a) the establishment of the characters of the children playing, and the contrast between them and the witches, wizards, gnomes, evil ones;

(b) the casting of the spell, and the resulting change in the children;

(c) the reversing of roles by the stealing of the magic instruments, and the ending situation.

Let us take each of these scenes in turn.

The children playing

This scene can be built up in various ways, partly organised and arranged by the teacher from the children's own ideas. A fairly literal kind of dance mime can be developed involving twos or threes, based on play actions which are familiar to

[1] See Ovid, *Metamorphoses*, translated by May M. Innis, Penguin Books 1955.

the class, such as ball-play, skipping, hopscotch, playing with hoops, tops, marbles and so on. All the preliminary work described in Chapter 8 will apply to this scene if it is developed in this way. An alternative is a more conventional style of group dance—circling, chain formations and so on—and this would need to be organised by the teacher. I prefer the less formal, more varied and lively contrasts provided by the first suggestion, though the final decision would depend upon the specific needs of the children at the time.

Meanwhile, the witches watch, either from one place (perhaps grouped in a corner) or from different places around the edges of the room. The watching should be active and a 'watching motif' developed, again either by the group or by individuals. Such motifs would be based on the ideas of watching (peering, peeping, gloating, laughing) and preparation for the casting of the spell.

For example, the starting position might be crouching on the floor, huddled close and small. The first part of the motif could be extending the body, reaching out, looking forward, eyes open wide, cymbals extended, slowly reaching into the area in front. The second part of the motif might develop from releasing the cymbals from the closed position, opening them out wide (soundlessly) spreading them as if casting a spell, and bringing them close back to the body to touch each other again. The third part of the motif might be a stepping, turning, huddled, laughing, surrounding movement, as if the witches were chuckling over the coming episode.

The rhythm for this sequence might be something like this: slow starting with a movement which reaches out, which is then repeated, followed by a pause, then an opening, spreading and lifting sequence at the same time, as if gaining height and power, then a pattern of quick stepping round—step, step, step, step, step, step, pause. This could be repeated in unison with others who are witches or wizards, so that there is a common motif and a common timing. Equally, it could be developed with individual variation from each witch or wizard according to his or her own personal choice.

After this has been repeated three, four, five, or however many times is decided, the witches' advance can be timed so that, at a given sign, they all reach their position of dominance together. This could be done by the witches staying in different places around the edges of the room, but watching each other and synchronising their movement; or they could form a closed-up group. This action would be the signal for some kind of change; the children could tire of their play and settle down in couples or threes or groups, yawn, stretch and lie down to sleep. The ending position for this section would then be a scattering of the children throughout the room, relaxed, lying on the floor. Surrounding them would be the witches looking from a distance, towering and dominating, cymbals held high, one in each hand, ready for scene two, which is the casting of the spell.

Casting the spell

The spell is cast as the climax of a build-up of magic. The magic is made by rubbing the two cymbals together, and this can be practised by all the children with the flat palms of the hands instead of the two cymbals. A motif needs to be developed for this section. It could be, for instance, stepping on a circular pathway around a child lying on the floor (for practice purposes have an imaginary child) rubbing the cymbals or the hands together as the stepping is going on, so there is a continuous scraping, rubbing sound accompanying the stepping. The witches would lift their legs high, step onto the toes, bend the body and gloat over the victim.

The next part of this motif could be a build-up in sound, in action and in the excitability of the witch, culminating in the great crash at the end. (This kind of phrase, which reaches a strong climax at the end, is known as an impactive phrase.) This phrase could start with the witches low near the floor, the position they adopted at the end of the circling; there they would gradually rise, lightly clashing the cymbals, grow in a crescendo phrase, lifting higher and higher and higher, and at a given signal crash the cymbals together high above the victim. The end position is of the witch looking down over the crouched victim.

The child who was asleep reacts; his body, which was relaxed, jerks, changes position, becomes grotesque and non-human. One witch will have to influence more than one child, so that various arrangements of groups could be worked out for any given class. For instance, the sequence of spell-making could be repeated three or four or five times, each time round a single child. At the end of the first phrase one particular child reacts. Then the focus of the witch changes to a new child and the whole sequence is repeated, and then on to the third and fourth. Or it could be arranged that one witch travels around all three or four victims. The spell would then affect the whole group of children at the end of the first phrase. At the repetition of the spell, all the children would move into a new, grotesque position. It is suggested that at this stage the children should keep their eyes closed, so that the change, the metamorphosis, happens during sleep, and they awake to find themselves changed, strange and different. After repeating this magic motif, the witches have completed their task, and can back away slowly, perhaps rubbing the cymbals together to keep the magic alive, and take up a position either in a group or again scattered round the room, placing the cymbals on the floor. Then they can rest, crouching, peering, looking, to see the result of their magic.

This would lead into the next part of the scene which would show how the children move in this new, strange shape. At this point the teacher might decide to bring in appropriate music, to make appropriate sounds on percussion, or to let the children themselves make sounds to accompany their movement. The grotesque, angular or twisted positions of the children lend themselves to jerky, distorted, harsh movement patterns and phrases. The accompaniment for this could be jerky noises, grunts, squeaks, sounds of a non-human nature from the children; it could be sounds in phrased patterns played on rattles, scrapers or discordant instruments; or it could be irregular discordant musical sequences. Whatever the sound accompaniment, it must gradually become fixed, clear and organised, so that by repetition the children know exactly how long they have and what movement phrases are expected from them.

One possibility is for the children to start a kind of grotesque, individual dance, balancing on different parts of

the body instead of the usual legs and feet, leaping into the
air in grotesque shapes and forms, turning, twisting, rolling,
tumbling, in as non-human, non-childlike a way as possible.
Young children enjoy this grotesque play, and they should be
encouraged gradually to select from the freely invented
sequences, and repeat exactly (or almost exactly) the
sequences they choose. For those children who are more
advanced, this section could be developed to show relationships between individuals, couples, or even groups, so that
there would be couples meeting, parting, turning together,
rolling together, meeting other couples, advancing, retreating,
parting, and so on. Once the length of this section is fixed the
children should become conscious and practised in their
exact movement patterns and sequences so that the ending of
the section can be anticipated.

During this grotesque dance, the witches or wizards have a
minor but active sequence of movement patterns and motifs
in the background. They congratulate themselves and watch
the children so that their attention is distracted from the
cymbals which they placed on the floor after casting the
spell. When the motifs for the witches are established (again,
either from the teacher's suggestion or by the children
developing a motif pattern) the witches go towards each
other, meeting, becoming absorbed in 'telling each other'
about the action they have done, and share a common
delight, circling, meeting, parting, laughing together. At the
same time as they leave the instruments on the floor, one
grotesque 'child' comes across a pair of cymbals and stands
still, silent, hovering over the cymbals. Each set of cymbals
can then be found by one child, who sees them, poises over
them and slowly, slowly, slowly dares to touch them. The
children pick them up and, as they do so, perhaps scrape
them on the floor to make a sign in sound to their comrades.
Their comrades are turned into stone, into a statue, held in
some grotesque position, listening, waiting. The witches,
caught away from their magic cymbals, are helpless, hypno-
tised and afraid. They too are turned into stone. The children
with the cymbals then carefully pick them up and their task
is to reverse the spell. This sequence is the transition into the
third and last scene.

The reversing of roles
The children who have the cymbals rub them on the floor, while the rest of the class hold the positions they took up at the end of the previous scene. The main action is then taken over by the children with cymbals who develop a motif for reversing the magic. This reversal, which can be worked out in discussion with the children, could involve a reversing of the rhythmical pattern: as the spell was cast by a crescendo phrase ending in a crash, it could be reversed by a crash gradually diminishing; if it was cast by rising from the floor to a high, towering position, it could be reversed by starting from a high position and sinking gradually down. Again, all the children could practise this as if they were holding the cymbals, but using the palms of their hands. They start low, imagining that are holding cymbals, and make a wide, lifting movement towards the crash which starts the sequence to undo the magic. Then they sink slowly down to the floor, rubbing the cymbals together or rattling them as they go, dying down.

The grotesque creatures respond to the lifting of the spell. At the first crash, they shudder, look at their own arms, legs, hands, bodies, and recognise how twisted and distorted they are. Gradually during the rattling or rubbing of the cymbals the spell is lifted; they unwind their arms and straighten them out, ease the twisting in their legs, their knees, their eyes, their faces, until they are straight, human children again. They look around and see the other children, recognise their playmates, and run to each other, perhaps forming three groups of ten or twelve children. Their delight is shown by circling and enclosing those children who have touched the magic instruments and by placing them in front of the group to show that they are the leaders.

Throughout this part, the witches or wizards are completely still, or they can slowly withdraw sinking, attempting to escape. Each of the groups of children advances towards the witches—menacing, attacking, firm and strong. The witches spread out, trying to escape. The children follow, surrounding them, and trap them inside a circle from which they cannot escape. The magic is still in the hands of the children, who develop a motif of dominance over the witches

and aggression towards them. According to the number of groups in which the children have collected, the ending will be in three, four, five groups with one or two witches in the centre of each circle. The motif of killing the witch can be developed in a sequence of three or four phrases—for instance, advancing and backing, advancing and backing, advancing and attacking, and kill. The witch can die agonisingly, silently, disappearing as if going through the floor, or making a hideous struggle, with appropriate sound, as he or she dies. The triumphant children surround the witch.

As the whole composition has been discussed, suggestions have been made at various points that the entire class could practise a particular sequence or motif. From experience it seems better that these motifs are developed as the story develops, rather than many lessons and weeks being spent on practising individual motifs which are then built up together into the finished product.

All the children should be given the opportunity to play various roles. There will be a clamour to be the witches. There will be a clamour to be the children who find the cymbals. All the children should know all the parts, although every child does not have to take every part on each occasion the composition is performed, and it can be allowed to develop slightly differently according to which children are in the leading roles on any particular occasion.

Nevertheless, if the children are to feel secure in a fixed composition of this sort, it must take a fixed form similar to that of a music composition, song or sequence. This means that all the children know what is happening, just as they might know all the different parts in part singing. The teacher is responsible for keeping the phrases fixed, regular in repetition, and for making sure that the transitions between the sections and phrases happen at the appropriate time. These transitions have to be learned, just as much as the main movement sequences, otherwise the whole composition becomes chopped up into a series of isolated parts. If there is really a 'logic' in the composition itself, then the movement sequences will develop one from the other.

If children are to develop a movement story of this length, they must be able not only to perform the actual movement motifs but also to remember in advance which sequence comes after the one they are taking part in at the moment. This is why compositions of this length and kind cannot, in fact, be successfully performed by very young infants. Movement memory develops, as all kinds of memory develop, through practice and experience. Just as the ability to write and read longer sentences and phrases is a sign of growing maturity, so the ability to master longer phrases of movement, and the accompanying sound patterns and transitions, is a sign of a child's development.

DISCOVERING PERCUSSION

A similar composition to that of the magic cymbals can be developed with young children who are discovering how to handle and play percussion instruments effectively and artistically. As previously discussed, sounds, including vocal sounds, are a very natural accompaniment to movement, and the young infant can progress from using his voice to playing a percussion instrument while moving and dancing. Some instruments are easier and should be used first; others are very much more difficult to play and move to at the same time. Easy ones are bells and rattles, and those instruments which can be held in the hand and are very little different from a slight extension of the body itself. The sounds happen because the rhythms of the body activate the bell or the rattle, just as the hands are activated as the child moves. Drums, cymbals and tuned instruments are much more difficult to play and require very subtle handling in order to create effective sound. A very young child with a drum will not be able to move easily with it, but will tend to stop moving and play the drum, his movement being mainly concentrated in his hands and arms. Therefore the teacher should put off the introduction of percussion with which the children move, until the appropriate time for the particular group. Children who have had experience of moving while playing bells and rattles, will find it easier than those who have had no experience at the early stages.

When the children are able to play the instrument reasonably efficiently while moving, one can set them to move in unison with its sound—for instance a shivery movement with the bells, angular staccato movement with the rattles, long, elongated continuous movement with gongs. Only after this experience can the formulated sequence of a very simple composition be attempted.

For example, imagine that the children see a pile of instruments in the centre of the room. They have never seen such objects before; they come from another land and another world, and they approach this pile of objects cautiously, with suspicion, with care, with respect. One child, more daring, might reach out and touch an instrument. It makes a sound, the children spin away, rolling, flying, tumbling, crawling, to get away from the sound, but nothing terrible happens. They look at the instruments; they seem harmless. The daring one creeps back again, either supported by the others or watched by them. He touches the instrument again. He springs away in fear, but not so far this time. He tries again: he dares to pick it up; he develops the sound, recognising that he has some control over it. It is not a 'being' which has control over him. He can play it; he can stop it; he can throw it down; he can pick it up again. He jumps with it, turns, puts it down, listens to it, and demonstrates that this object might be a servant to man and not a power over him. At some place in this sequence, the other children recognise that there are other objects which they might try. Another child creeps up, picks up another kind of instrument, plays with it and develops a sequence. A third one, a fourth one, a fifth one, follow and with a whoop of joy the whole of the rest of the class swoops to the instruments. Each child picks up one instrument and takes it away, rolling, curling, jumping, flying to a space on his own. In playing alone with the instrument, sequences reflecting the sound which the child makes on the instrument can be developed. This will involve travelling, turning, opening and closing the body, flying, falling and rolling, and some time should be given for the children to develop a particular phrased sequence which is repeated.

In making the composition, the children will gradually come to know their own instrument and will have placed it appropriately in the centre; they will anticipate the order in which they pick them up; they will develop movement motifs to accompany the actions of the first ones who pick up the instruments; and they will be able to take the instrument away and develop their rhythmical sequence into a pattern of, for instance, three or four phrases. The teacher plays a vital role in ordering and calling attention to all these stages.

From this point, many development are possible. If the children are old enough and experienced enough with percussion they can develop this individual work and elaborate it into meeting a partner, into a question-and-answer situation in movement. No words are spoken, but it is as if one partner says 'Look at my instrument—it makes me jump—boom, boom, boom, boom!' The reply is 'Look at my instrument—it makes me shiver—brrr!' The composition would continue with alternating sequences from each partner, each choosing a definite action—'It makes me travel like this' or 'It makes me jump like this' or 'It makes me spin around like this' or 'It makes me fall to the floor like this' or 'It makes me very very quietly lift up and spread out and drop down.' Another idea would be to meet a partner and exchange instruments. You show the partner the one you have—'Look, I have a drum! It makes me jump and step and stamp!'—'Look, I have a clapper! It makes me be jerky, angular, staccato! Shall we change round?' Perhaps this could be expressed by circling around one another, holding out the instruments and, at a given moment, exchanging them and going off, moving in phrases of movement of a different character, according to the instrument.

The ending of such a dance play for the children could be the security of having achieved a new extension to their lives over which they have control when the instruments are mastered. It could be that at some outside sound, such as a gong, a drum or a whistle, they become afraid and return the instruments to the centre and creep away. Or it could be that, at some point in time, the instruments, as if having a will of their own, begin to pull the children back to the centre and make them put them down, so that it is as if the instruments are animated by some sort of force within themselves and cannot ultimately be mastered and taken over.

It is helpful to the children if they try out together the

different kinds of ending which are possible, so that when they come to make their own ending they can choose from a range and variety of sequences. This will ensure that the ending is in the same style as the rest of the composition. Whatever the ending to the dance play, the children must be able to repeat it precisely, exactly and with content.

MECHANICAL CREATURES OR TOYS OR DOLLS

Young children often enter into the play of 'being' and 'not being'. They become a wild animal ('I'm a lion—a tiger') or a mechanical toy or object (I'm a train—a bomber—a machine— a rocket') and yet fully realise that they are not the animal or object. They absorb the characteristics of the being they become, and creep or stalk through the jungle, chug, or zoom, or click or shoot. This kind of play usually involves many kinds of metamorphoses which the children manage without worrying about the literalness of it all. They change roles at will, die or revive themselves, become the murdered or the victim. Usually their voice accompaniments are vivid, accurate and expressive, synchronised with their movement phrases.

In choosing a theme of mechanical objects, the teacher is entering into this world which is the child's own, and it depends upon the skill used in presenting the ideas, whether the children can accept and use them, and translate them into movement forms.

As an example, the theme of clockwork machines will be discussed here. In the very elementary stage, a young child can represent parts of the machine with parts of his own body. It is more difficult to fit two or more bodies together to make a larger machine, for the child must not only be aware of his own body, the parts in action and how they relate to each other, but must also observe the movements of another child and synchronise with them. Even first- and second-year infants can synchronise simple actions like lifting and sinking in opposition to a partner, but it is too much to expect more than repeated single ideas.

In using the theme with older children, the teacher can expect and provoke inventiveness; for instance 'whell-like' movements; 'piston-like' movements, 'cog-like' movements, or 'shuttle-like' movements can be made, and two, three or four children can be expected to work together. A very successful idea for middle-school juniors can be that of clocks. It is worth taking the trouble to provide opportunities for the children to look at various kinds of clock and take them to pieces so that they can get to know their mechanisms. Slow-ticking old grandfather pendulum clocks have a different character from the spritely watch or tiny desk clock. Elegant period clocks contrast with alarm clocks, and of course cuckoo clocks are great favourites.

The more the whole body action can be involved, the more the mechanism becomes 'alive'. This involvement might be an exaggerated attitude of the body, held in a position to support more isolated gestures, or it might be actual rolling, turning, bending or stretching of the whole body. Without doubt, the children will be helped in their movement patterns by making noises—clicks or ticks or whirlings and the striking of the hour or the cuckoo sounds. The sounds helpd to phrase the action.

After the study of mechanisms, the children can experiment with a small 'machine' idea. The first lesson will perhaps not extend beyond the building of a piece of clockwork between two children, stressing the sound phrases as well as the movement phrases.

The next lesson might be devoted to working in a small group, making the decision as to the type of clock, its sounds, its mechanisms, and its shape and action.

The third lesson could be the culmination in which the theme is finalised. The children can work in small, separate groups, or the whole class can cooperate in a 'family' of clocks with simultaneous actions. In a composition involving the whole class, the addition of a story might be suggested by the children. For example, the clock man winds his clocks in sequence, with big keys, or little keys, with hard pressure or slight, according to the clock; he watches them with satisfaction as they tick regularly on; he falls asleep and dreams of them coming to life; they go faster anf faster and finally explode, or they disintegrate into tangled pieces; parts might become animated and run wild and attack him or surround him or lead him in a dance; he wakes to find it a dream.

Stories like this hold the clocks together and help to phrase and form the action. Many such sequences can be devised: the clock pieces can be playful, menacing, stupid or acrobatic according to the choice of the class or the teacher.

The end product should be a 'clock' dance which can be repeated precisely, and in which both the action and the sound are enjoyable to perform. More advanced classes can find appropriate music, and start lesson three from the musical form, following the phrases, and composing the action to suit the phrases of the music.

SUMMARY

In making compositions, one must decide what kind of meaning is being sought; for instance, it may be the experience of being as mechanical and 'non-human' as possible, or of making or responding to magical influences. When the meaning is clear (and it may only become clear gradually as the composition is developed) the style of movement will evolve, as being the best possible way of expressing the meaning. This style might vary from the clear shaping, patterning and rhythm in what is often termed 'abstract' movement (although it is intensely anchored in a 'concrete' body) to a more realistic portrayal of the idea through the use of characters and mimetic action. The same idea presented to a class can be developed in groups, each evolving its own style, or by the teacher who gives direction and guidance which limits the choice of style. In planning the presentation of an idea or theme, the teacher should take this difference into account and recognise the value of both approaches. Sometimes the major responsibility rests with the teacher, and the class have the security of being held and supported without too much being left to them: sometimes the choice and decision is with the children, who will then certainly need some help and guidance in the development of the style.

10 *Ritual Compositions*

While there are many possible variations in the kind of composition which can be called ritualistic, there are certain common elements, notably that the theme or idea will be of universal interest and that the form will be fixed and repeated in all essential details each time it is performed. Themes such as hunting, cultivating the land, or worship, take many forms. As has been pointed out already, many rituals are connected with events of individual and tribal importance: with birth, death, coming of age or marriage; with seasonal activities, magical propitiations to the gods, appeasement, offerings, worship; and with the enactment of traditional stories and myths and of historic events.

Hunting rituals are of the most primitive kind, relating to the period of man's evolution before he become a cultivator of the land. Many tribes retained these rituals, and performed them to ensure a good hunt, perhaps partly hoping for an actual kill, but also recognising a deeper significance in the act of hunting prey. Desmond Morris[1] explains how modern man retains the hunting instinct and his need for ritualising its performance.

Two examples of ritual dances are discussed in this chapter, based on hunting and on the idea of 'Mother Earth'.

THE HUNTING RITUAL

The hunting ritual can be divided into five main sections or scenes:

Scene 1: Stalking the prey
Scene 2: Seeing and concentrating attention on the victim
Scene 3: Attack and killing the victim
Scene 4: Dragging away the victim
Scene 5: Celebration of victory.

[1] Desmond Morris, *The Naked Ape*, Jonathan Cape 1967.

Scene 1: Stalking the prey

Preparation for this work can be done with the children stepping lightly, cautiously, perhaps slowly 'as if going through the jungle'. Clear phrasing should be given: 'Step, step, step, step, peer round, stop!' By repeating such a phrase a few times, the children can catch the rhythm of it and they will begin to link the end of one phrase (where the pause is) to the beginning of the next phrase. A drum rhythm, not just a beat, will help to phrase the action, as well as to set the mood.

When practising this phrase, attention should be given to those parts of the body that are particulary important. For instance, in stepping, one must consider the careful placing of the feet, precisely and exactly in position. The children must take care not to step on twigs or objects which would make a sound. In pausing, the body is still and all movement is with the eyes and head, peering first to one side and then to the other. Then the whole body is poised silently for a moment before the phrase is repeated. Changes of direction, so that each phrase is aimed towards a different position in the room, give variety and enable the class to make criss-crossing patterns. When the children, working as individuals, are familiar with this pattern they can work together in pairs, either side by side or one behind the other. In making the actual composition, one must decide whether all the children are moving all the time, or whether individual children (or couples, or small groups) are moving at different times, so that the position of the non-moving children is held through the phrase of movement of the others.

At a given moment, after, say, five or six phrases, one couple or one individual sees the animal. This event marks the end of the first scene and the transition into the second section of the ritual.

Scene 2: Seeing the victim

The first child (or pair of children) catch sight of the victim. Perhaps they edge forwards or upwards, or drop to the floor, or make some other sudden change in movement, and then hold still. This draws the attention of the other children.

Now the composition may be developed in a number of

different ways. Either all the children concentrate on the animal, building up behind the first child to have seen it, so that he becomes the leader; or many animals are seen. In the latter case, the timing is taken over by each small group, perhaps not even each group at the same time. The expression of concentration upon the victim comes from the focus of the eyes, and from the body, poised in stillness in a strongly gripped stance. Moving towards the victim may develop as a whole-group movement in unison, or it may be that one child goes forward in one short phrase, another follows in another phrase, another follows him, and so on. The phrases are built up to a climax. It is important for the children to decide exactly where the animal is, so that concentrated attention can be held on a specific spot. If they imagine that the animal is moving, the whole group slowly changes its focus of attention as the animal passes by, or moves above or beside them. This is an example of a group movement in unison. It forms the transition into Scene 3—the attack.

Scene 3: Attack and killing the victim

Again, the attack can be organised in small groups, each taking its attacking motif in unison in the group, or it can be organised so that the whole class, supported by an outer rhythm, attacks together. Whatever the organisation of the phrases, the common element here is that the phrase starts with a preparation, and is built up into a dynamic action, culminating in the throwing of the spear, stone, club, or whatever it is the children are handling. This motif should be repeated a few times so that the idea of attacking is emphasised before the kill is made. If it is a child playing the part of the beast which is being hunted, the response of the children to the animal will have to be worked out together with the teacher. The animal may try to fly or run away, or it may be so caught and surrounded by different groups of hunters that escape is impossible and it quickly dies. This leads to the next scene.

Scene 4: Dragging away the victim

When the animal is seen to be dead, the children approach,

prepare, and drag it away. Thus, it is symbolically moved from the place of death to the tribe's encampment. The pulling and dragging action is again a repetitive working action, involving strong, firm, body-centred movement. When the children arrive at a new place in the room, which can be imagined as the place of sacrifice or the centre of their village, they celebrate their achievement. Transition from the dragging action to the dance-celebration scene can be made immediately and very dramatically, and is particularly helped here by external rhythm, probably on a drum.

Scene 5: Celebration of victory

Leaping, jumping, whirling with rhythmically exciting phrases, leaping over the dead animal, circling round it, stamping, spreading out, advancing, retreating, jumping, and even whirling and falling away, provide the climax of the whole ritual. If this is to be an activity performed totally in unison, the teacher will need to help the children by asking them the following questions: Who is making the jumps at any one moment? Which individual or group is leaping over the animal? What happens to the children, at the other side of the animal, who are receiving the jumping child or children? How is the circling round the animal to be developed? Is it, for instance, to be with stamping feet, clapping hands, or whirling? How does the grouping develop to a climax and concluding position?

Certainly, for beginner teachers, it is easier to organise the whole class into one large composition with a fairly free adaptation of the movement by each child within the set phrase, than it is to allow varied rhythmical developments in each group. In order to be able to use this freer approach, the children have to be very experienced in holding on to their own rhythms, their own phrases and their own actions. Whether any particular class is ready for this can only be assessed by the teacher at the time.

Obviously, the drum is the best instrument for much of the accompaniment to this sequence or dance. Nevertheless, rattles, shakers or clappers may be involved at any one time, and it is a good opportunity for the building up of rhythmical sound phrases by the children themselves, if they are experienced enough in handling percussion to do this. Given such a basis, some classes might like to prepare their own accompaniment, record it, and later use it for their actual movement. Other classes will be at the stage where they depend on the teacher to hold the rhythmical phrases steady for them.

MOTHER EARTH

This composition is conceived as a group dance for any number of people, with a minimum of five.

The scenes here are envisaged as:

1   Individuals awakening and growing, pushing away from the earth (being born);
2   Opening out of the self and meeting others while also being one with the earth.
3   Working with others in working actions (scything, digging, hoeing, etc.);
4   Rejoicing, in small groups, as small tribes or units of individuals working together, and achieving satisfaction from working close to the earth;
5   Offering, involving lifting and carrying the fruits of the earth, processing and making offerings to Mother Earth herself;
6   Circling in tribute, in joy and with excitement, with the whole group acting in unison.

Scene 1: Awakening and growing

All the children are individually scattered about the room, lying on the floor as though asleep. In a series of phrases repeated three times, a slow pushing action follows and a kind of throbbing comes into the body.

The idea of this motif is the strong pushing away from the earth of the individual, in order to be born and to be separate from the earth. In the organisation of this motif, all the children might move together. However, if there is a large number, it is helpful to group the children into four sections, so that one section grows in the first phrase and holds the position, the second section grows in the second, and the third in the third. In the fourth section, all the children join together and rise to a kneeling position. The pulse or beat at the end of each short phrase is a thumping on the ground. At the beginning, while children are lying on the ground, the fists will make the thumping. Later, when they kneel or stand, the feet will make the pulsating beat. The next series of phrases will bring the children to standing positions, and this is a growing all together, although each child is still an individual and they are spread out in the room. The movement is slow, sustained and strong, struggling to get away from the earth which holds the children down and binds them, until the moment of finding that they are free from the earth, and that the centre of importance has shifted from the earth itself to the centre of their own bodies. They can then lift, stretch, and extend their bodies in a way which no animal can, reaching up and aspiring, and the exhilaration of this sends the class into a whirling, vibrating turn.

Scene 2: 'Opening out'

This scene happens on the horizontal plane, and contains a phrased motif of opening, first to one side, and then to the other, and a turning around to see others. It is repeated several times. Perhaps the first time, it will be small and hardly extend in space. The hands are turned outwards, the fingertips pointing outwards as if seeking the outer world. The turn is an opening turn, for the body is 'opening out' and thereby becoming more vulnerable to the outside world, as well as more able to make contact with it by taking the initiative.

After these motifs are developed (in size, intensity and speed) the children break into a travelling motif of excitement, where the legs and feet become important, and where the fingertips are extended forwards to meet another person. It is a first meeting. The two touch finger tips momentarily, and the effect is like an electric shock from which they spring away, turn to a new place in the room and meet a new partner. The same thing happens again and again. Eventually, each child remains with his partner. The contacts are no longer fleeting but more permanent, and not only are the finger tips touching but the hands grip, press or develop some new hold on each other, before the two turn together to emphasise being united. This moment ends the scene.

Scene 3: Working actions

Details of some working actions, particularly related to cultivating the soil, were given in Chapter 4.

In practising this third section, all the children should individually rehearse the˙ kinds of action sequences from which they may be asked to make a personal selection. For instance, they will practise such actions as digging the soil, hoeing, reaping, scything, scattering seeds, stooking, and so on. The class then forms itself into small groups which develop these rhythmical actions in sequences and work together in unison. Probably, the most helpful formation is for them all to face in the same direction.

Some of the motifs lend themselves to travelling movements, and the floor patterns need to be worked out. Other motifs will include actions which require staying in one place. The transition from the second scene of the composition to these working actions must be considered. How do the couples join together in small groups? This may involve a lively awareness on their part that work has to be done, which initiates a jump, a swoop together to meet a new group, and a gathering up of implements and the immediate start on the working action; or it can be a more sustained development of the working actions gradually through the group, enacted by one couple starting the action sequence, then another couple joining in, and so on.

Scene 4: Rejoicing

This scene develops and echoes the first individual whirling, but now the children are rejoicing in small groups, the working-action groups they have just been in. The motif here picks up the stamping, throbbing beat and the whirling, turning exuberance, whirling round and round and round, bang, bang, bang and on the floor! This phrase is repeated two, three, four, or five times, according to the needs of the composition. Each group practises the motif, but there is no need for them all to start at the same time. From the working actions, the motif can be developed by the formation of a circle and the rhythm in the whole group will then arise from the differently accented phrasing of each smaller group. In other words, the beating on the floor will be maintained by one group while the others are rising or circling or sinking ready to beat on the floor. An irregular rhythm will arise spontaneously where the accents are taken up by one group after another, if each starts the same motif at different times.

Scene 5: Offering

A transition is required from the circling or beating of the previous scene to the lifting of offerings, the fruits of work. It is best to take this transition as a floor motif, where the children are kneeling. The children turn towards a common direction once more, lifting their offerings and carrying them in procession. Again, the movements need to be fixed so that criss-crossing pathways are made in the room and the processing has a more formal quality. As indicated in Chapter 4, the method of lifting and carrying which is a type of mimetic movement, is dependent on the imagined objects. If the objects are very small and delicate, the movement will be fine, sensitive and careful; if they are very heavy and bulky, the movement will be gross, extended and firm, and will require getting the weight of the body underneath to lift— probably with both hands. If the object is very large then perhaps more than one child will be needs to lift it. Practise is necessary for lifting and carrying imagined objects in unison, and will include the children's adapting themselves to the shape and weight which is imagined. After the procession, each group makes the transition to the offering section of the composition by focusing towards the centre of the room, approaching the centre, lifting the offering high into the air and bringing it down. It is placed back on Mother Earth. This symbolic action may be done in unison by the whole group offering at the same moment, or, perhaps more interestingly it can be done in sequence. If the sequence is not too mechanically organised, an impressive group rhythm can be built up—approaching, lifting, placing, and withdrawing. The withdrawing should be played as a backing away from the centre of the circle so that the groups arrive at the outside edges, ready for the final scene.

Scene 6: Circling in tribute

Stamping again with gaiety, and repeating and echoing the

previous circling, the children once more relate themselves to the earth. Their bodies are bent and crouched, but are now focused forward upon the offerings. The action is that of advancing and retiring in rhythmical phrases, one group advancing as another group is retiring, and cross-phrasing each other. Finally, when these sequences have built to a vibrating climax, in keeping with the whole scene, a unison advance is made to the centre. This meeting together in the centre culminates in an ending which has a single, slowly opening phrase. This concluding phrase is not a wide-spreading opening, but rather one where the children are representing their absorption, both in themselves as individuals in a circle, and in the goods which they have offered. The mood is one of stillness and containment.

It is important to stress the transition between the motifs within each scene, the transitions between the scenes themselves, and the precision of the phrasing. This composition was originally worked with parts of the music from the *Missa Luba*, which lends itself to ritualistic, repetitive, throbbing, earth-bound movement. The whole composition arose from a consideration of the Mother Earth theme. The meaning captures symbolically the ideas of struggling to get away from the mother, finding the self, and recognising the special qualities and aspirations of man.

This aspiring is essentially represented in his lifting himself up and away from the earth, and in forming a new link with the community. He is not alone but needs other people, just as he must recognise the remember his basic rootedness in the earth itself. The need for relationships between people, both in work and play, is brought out and symbolised in unison movements. Such movements in the working, worship and offering actions, emphasise that strength comes from people being together and cooperating. Celebration is a communal activity. The earth is the mother, and all the banging, stamping, and beating of the earth symbolises touch, and the being in touch, which is retained throughout life. The whirling and turning represents mobility, and excitability. Cooperative effort ensures achievement of the fruits of the earth; But some of the harvest must be offered back (as in the Harvest Festival; see Chapter

4). The celebration is made in the large, symbolic circle.

Motifs occurring throughout include

(a) Circling   In this composition, circling is symbolic of unison, of eternal movement and equality; it also symbolises enclosing and embracing, and excluding. Circling occurs alone in whirling, in pairs turning together, and in small groups and larger ones when the whole community is united.

(b) Touching, beating, hammering the earth   This motif symbolises that man's roots are in the earth. If he should lose contact with the earth, he cannot live. He returns to his roots regularly and must understand how best he can work with nature—not only by working and tilling the ground, but also by entering into the rhythmical sequences which nature provides. Thus, pulse and beat occur repetitively throughout the whole composition: first, alone, when the hands bang on the floor, and the feet stamp; secondly, in small-group motifs, when work is over, and there is time for relaxation; and thirdly, after the unison offering, when celebration again recaptures the link with the earth.

(c) Aspiration   In this motif, the children feel themselves in charge of their own movement and bodies, and are able to pull away from the earth while yet keeping their feet anchored. They aspire upwards in a way that no animal can. This basic movement occurs in the dance in individual motifs and when the couples dance together. It is repeated in the final offering before the placing of the fruits of the earth in the centre of the room. The offerings are held high, so linking the heavens and the earth.

(d) Alternating phrases of vibration and sustaining   These phrases are motifs of increase and decrease, where the inner effort of excitement and pulsating life grows, even to bursting point. A contrast is therefore made with the quieter, more contained phrases of those movements which realise the centre of the self, and the relationship of the self to the earth and to other people.

(e) Joining together   The motifs of joining and meeting develop from those of individual growth. The development is that of first meeting one partner, forming small groups, and later becoming a part of the large unit, just as each one of us

is an individual, yet also in relationship with, at some times, one other person, and at others a small group, perhaps the family unit, and again with a larger unit, such as the school, city or country. The larger unit can symbolise the whole of mankind.

(f) Stillness The stillness is a living stillness, where the children do not stop 'moving', but rather retain a movement within the body without actually moving about from place to place. The movement is held with tension, concentration and absorption. Sometimes it occurs between two active motifs, as a transition, when the necessary change of focus is helped by an inner stillness and containment, following on from the first action and in preparation for the next. At the end of the composition, the group is left in stillness, but still vibrating, aware and alive.

SUMMARY: PRINCIPLES OF COMPOSITION

Eight examples of compositions have been given: Magnetism; Ball game; Fight; Magic cymbals; Percussion; Mechanical toys—clockwork; Hunting ritual; Mother Earth.

The first three compositions are for couples and the remainder are for small or large groups. I had originally meant to give many more examples, but found that to describe a composition in words takes up much more space than does a decription in notation, so I have had to reduce the number. I hope that the various attempts to describe the dances or compositions will stimulate teachers to try out their own ideas.

Although it is impossible to summarise the process of composing a dance, the following points must be considered, irrespective of the method of composition chosen. The order of consideration will vary according to the composer, the group of children and the theme.

(a) The theme, the idea and the 'meaning'; and the title which captures the theme as nearly as possible;

(b) The scenes or sections of movement (like chapters in a book) necessary to formulate the meaning;

(c) The motifs which are involved in each scene, and how they relate one to another (transitions, motif development, etc);

(d) The groupings of the children; the individuals, the couples, the small or large groups necessary to capture the meaning within the motif;

(e) The overall 'arrangement' of the groups; the patterning of stationary or moving groups;

(f) The quality or rhythm of each motif; and how the resulting mood is achieved in 'effort' phrases (see Part Three for description of 'effort') with subtleties of increase and decrease of time, accent, restrained or free flow, etc.;

(g) How the body is used by each individual; which part takes the lead, what shape it makes, how it grows or shrinks, etc.;

(h) How the individual body relates to the group 'body' or shape; in joining, touching, huddling, spreading, etc.;

(i) How the sound (percussion, voice sounds, music, etc.) is related to the movement phrases; which phrases are taken in silence and which are accompanied; whether the sound-rhythms arise from the movement-rhythms, or whether the movement adapts to the previously composed sound or music.[2]

The choice of themes may, as suggested earlier, arise from any activity, interest or study on the part of the children, or it may be inspired by the teacher.

The value of such movement compositions has already been discussed and there is no doubt that when children participate in a large group dance or dramatic composition, they have a unique opportunity to develop their individual potential within the group experience. The composed form of a dance or dramatic sequence or mime provides the structure and security within which the individual can give his personal nuances of movement—his particular way of performing a given movement phrase or pattern, which is a re-living of the experience each time. This can be compared with the re-creating of a piece of music each time it is played or sung.

[2] For further help on movement practice and study see M. North, *A Guide to Movement Study and Teaching*.

III Understanding Children through observing their Movement

11 *Educational and Therapeutic Use of Movement*

An understanding of movement can be developed by teaching others, by participating in movement sessions, and by study and analysis. Intellectual knowledge about movement should not be scorned, although it needs a particular kind of understanding for it to be useful to the teacher.

Whether or not the relationships between movement capacities, on the one hand, and IQ or personality traits, on the other, are interdependent or are both dependent on some other fundamental property of the person, it seems clear that the association is not fortuitous. There is no proof that movement education or therapy can influence the personality or affect the intelligence, but many teachers and therapists give convincing accounts of the benefits of movement to their pupils and patients. A detailed discussion of the values of art education and therapy—the visual arts, music, and literature, as well as the art of movement—would be out of place here, but there are three points which are perhaps relevant.

The first point is that the educative or therapeutic effect comes from the art, that is, from the synthesising, formulating and symbolic processes, and not from what is loosely called 'freedom of expression', which usually amounts to nothing more than a self-indulgent sentimentality! This has been particularly demonstrated in movement where drum rhythms or music are used to stimulate a 'freeing up' of patients or pupils, to encourage them to move how they like. Usually, those patients or pupils who can do this freely are the ones who do not need encouragement in this 'emotional swimming'; those who cannot indulge in such 'freedom' could perhaps benefit from an ease and increase in their free flow and in a reduction of tension, if they could do it. So it appears that, either way, this so-called method of treatment or teaching has little to commend it.

This is not to deny that all art involves an element of self-expression. But education or therapy through art-media go beyond this personal expression; they help the participant to form his ideas, feelings and sensations into a disciplined wholeness, where symbolic actions (sounds, shapes, colours, and so on) becomes the vehicle of expression and transforms what is purely personal into something beyond the initial improvisation. Such work in movement can be individual or it can involve group relationships; it can be, and at the beginning is, limited, simple and elementary, but the process is the same as for the creation of any piece of art.

The second point is that much of the weakness of both teaching and therapeutic work in movement can be traced to insufficient knowledge and experience in the medium, together with a lack of understanding of the relationships which exist between personality and movement characteristics. This section attempts to show some of the more 'respectable' ways in which deeper investigation of movement could be developed, if and when there are sufficient practitioners who are prepared to master the subject. Any artist must dedicate himself to the craft as well as to the expression of his art.

The third point to be made is that further studies developed on lines similar to this one could begin to illustrate the profound effect which might be achieved with pupils and patients, if the subtle, psychosomatic relationships become clearer. As in the understanding of any art, the intuitive and feeling responses to the art, and to other people, are not to be underestimated. This sensitivity and awareness will be heightened by increased knowledge, that is, by knowing through experience and relating study to the experience, as distinct from knowing about the subject merely from reading a book or accumulating information.

As there seems a high level of correlation between measured IQ and movement capacity, it is difficult to avoid supposing that movement ability is more than a measurable or practical activity. Indeed, man's cognitive functions appear to be highly dependent on (or, alternatively, result in) a wide range of movement capacities, and probably they are so interrelated that there is no simple cause and result. What has been inference, from general observation, can now be supported. Einstein's statement[1] that his thinking occurred in optical and kinaesthetic images of movement can be understood quite literally as to mean that movement, of the qualitative nature described in shadow movements and body attitudes, actually 'contains' cognitive elements, as well as feeling, intuition and sensation. Freud's statement that 'thinking is experimental action with only a slight expenditure of energy' describes the same phenomena, but this has not been illustrated so clearly before now. Piaget also recognised that cognition starts at the sensory motor level, but what is now perhaps more obviously recognisable is that cognition is interdependent with complex movement patterns and combinations. It has always been recognised by movement specialists that space effort, or the ability to make shapes and forms in space, is linked with cognition. What was not so clearly seen before, was how much *all* movement capacities and their interlinking, pattern-forming content (which includes the transitions we have mentioned) is related to cognitive processes. Being able to formulate and make patterns and forms, to make leaps or bridges between ideas, thoughts and feelings, is all linked with man's developing cognitive functions.

Desmond Morris says: 'At the pre-verbal stages, before the massive machinery of symbolic, cultural communication has bogged us down, we rely much more on tiny movements, postural changes and tones of voice than we need to in later life.'[2] In describing a child or chimpanzee discovering that he can make visual patterns, he says: 'During the months that follow, these simple shapes are combined, one with another, to produce simple abstract patterns. A circle is cut through by a cross, the corners of a square are joined by diagonal lines. This is the vital stage that precedes the very first pictorial representations. In the child this great breakthrough comes in the second half of the third year or the beginning of the fourth. In the chimpanzee it never comes . . . the animal continues to grow but its pictures do not.' These comments

[1] J. Hadamard, *An Essay on the Psychology of Invention in the Mathematics Field*, Princeton University Press, 1954.

[2] *The Naked Ape*

from a zoologist pinpoint the previous statements relating intelligence, or cognitive function, to organisation, formulation and recognition of these forms. These functions of cognition are the prerogative of man,[3] and are revealed in all his arts. The exploratory stage is the early 'play' of the infant, the forming of these exploratory lines, movements, shapes, and words into art-forms is for the developing man, who now in a deeper sense needs to retain his capacity for 'play'.

Education and therapy, therefore, can claim to go beyond the early infant stage only if these formative elements are developed, and the child or adult is led beyond the stage of 'doodling'.

Teachers or therapists who leave their pupils or patients to improvise movement to music or rhythm are relying on that limited exploratory stage, which may play a valuable part in the context of a whole session but is not necessarily educative or therapeutic in itself. The whole range of movement potential must ultimately be incorporated in efficient teaching; neither the over-free, 'non-conscious' elements alone, as it used so often in the so-called 'relaxation' approach, nor rhythmically accented hypnotic drumming sessions, nor the over-conscious 'intellectual' approach, will suffice when used continuously and without development and form.

The gradual build-up of movement or kinaesthetic memory, which a baby begins to acquire and which continues throughout life, can be encouraged, enlarged and sensitised through the practice of the art of movement, just as a musical memory is developed through practice. This kind of memory, which is sensitive, related to past events, and imaginatively stimulated, is probably also an aid to cognitive feeling and intuitive functions. Certainly there seem to be grounds for recognising that kinaesthetic awareness plays a large part in our memory systems.

[3] Rudolph Laban, whose contribution is discussed later in this chapter, recognised what must be quite evident to everyone, but still has not been studied in detail, that each species of animal has its own range of movement effort in space, each highly specialised and efficient; but man has the whole range, less specialised but wider and richer and more capable of development than any other animal. It seems that such a detailed study of animal species would be highly revealing as to the stage of development of each. (See R. Laban, *Mastery of Movement on the Stage*, Macdonald & Evans 1950.)

Could it be that the refined observation of movement would allow us to see the whole area of intelligence and cognition in a new light? In addition, to those personality traits which are claimed to be discernible through movement, it appears that we can also discern cognitive ability. It is uncertain how early in a child's life some kind of prediction of intelligence can be made, but by movement observation, at least no reliance is placed on vocabulary or verbal understanding, nor is there in the same way a 'test' situation, and these factors may in the future prove to be advantageous.

The final word on the significance of human movement is given by R. G. Collingwood[4] who has discussed language in all its forms. He gives forceful support by inference to the inclusion of the art of movement in education and therapy, and to the notion that personalities reveal themselves (individually and racially) through their movement. What he writes also provides a justification for research into human movement for the sake of increasing our self-knowledge.

I said that 'the dance is the mother of all languages'—this demands further explanation. I meant that every kind or order of language (speech, gesture and so forth) was an off-shoot from an original language of total bodily gesture. This would have to be a language in which every movement and every stationary poise of every part of the body has the same kind of significance which movements of the vocal organs possess in a spoken language. A person using it would be speaking with every part of himself. Now, in calling this an 'original' language, I am not indulging (God forbid) in that kind of *a priori* archaeology which attempts to reconstruct man's distant past without any archaeological data. I do not place it in the remote past. I place it in the present. I mean that each one of us, whenever he expresses himself, is doing so with his whole body, and is actually talking in this 'original' language of total bodily gesture. This may seem absurd. Some people, we know, cannot talk without waving their hands and shrugging their shoulders and waving their bodies about, but others can

[4] R.G. Collingwood, *The Principles of Art*, Clarendon Press 1938; paperback edition 1965.

and do. That is no objection to what I am saying. Rigidity is a gesture, no less than movement. If there were people who never talked unless they were standing stiffly at attention, it would be because that gesture was expressive of a permanent emotional habit which they felt obliged to express concurrently with any other emotion they might happen to be expressing. This 'original' language of total bodily gesture is thus the one and only real language, which everybody who is in any way expressing himself is using all the time. What we call speech and other kinds of language are only parts of it which have undergone specialised development; in this specialised development they never come altogether detached from the parent organism.

This parent organism is nothing but the totality of our motor activities, raised from the psychical level to the conscious level. It is our bodily activity of which we are conscious. But that which is raised from the psychical level to the conscious level is converted by the work of consciousness from the impression to the idea, from object to sensation to object of imagination. The language of total bodily gesture is thus the motor side of our total imaginative experience.

12 *Movement Characteristics and Personality Traits*

This chapter involves the teacher's ability to observe the children, and ✦to understand what they are 'saying' at a non-verbal level.

General observation during lessons

During a movement class, every good teacher responds to the children by both listening and observing what they do. The teacher who only stimulates the class, and does not recognise the children's responses to the stimulus, is unable to progress in any meaningful way. (As I have indicated, this is the major criticism against being taught by mechanical devices, like the radio.) Meaningful teaching requires a constant picking up of responses, and the making of a new response by the teacher. This can be imagined in the shape of a figure eight, which continually alternates between giving and receiving.

What to look for

The teacher must first of all recognise whether the class has fulfilled the task which was set. For example, if the task is 'to shrink away to nothing' accompanied by a particular sound phrase, then the observation will be focused on whether the task is fulfilled in the following ways:

    (a) Bodily: is the movement throughout the body, or limited to one part? Could the shrinking away be more intense, if parts of the body actually touched, and so on?

    (b) Qualitatively: is the movement timed with the given phrase, and is the quality or expression appropriate to the sound?

    (c) Spatially: is there, for instance, a 'disappearance', by the body taking up less space, shrinking within

itself, and becoming unaware of the space around
it?

(d) In relationship to others: is there a leaving behind,
turning away and breaking off from others into
oneself, or does the whole group remain a single
entity, shrinking away together, still keeping the
contact?

With the help of these observations, the teacher can
encourage, coach or emphasise according to the children's
achievement.

At the stage of producing whole compositions, the particular movement phrases will be developed in this way, and in
addition the transitions between the phrases will be developed.

Observing individual children

This kind of class observation, then, is part of a teacher's
normal skill and technique. In addition, it will be recognised
that every child can fulfil the task in a personal and
individual way. These personal differences in movement can
be a valuable source of information for the teacher.

Usually, such knowledge about the child is acquired by a
teacher in a spontaneous and intuitive way. Comments about
a child's 'clumsiness', 'precision', 'care', 'vitality' or 'dullness',
have connections with the way the child moves, not only
with the pieces of work he produces.

It is possible to supplement or extend this capacity for
natural observation through study and practice, and some
interesting research has been done with both junior-age
children and with babies, which makes very specific links
between movement characteristics and personality traits.[1]

Without reaching the stage of being a highly skilled
practitioner who uses the method as a diagnostic tool, the
teacher can do more than make purely intuitive observations.
He can learn a great deal in the classroom if he is willing to
spend some time and practice in improving his observational

[1] M. North, *Personality Assessment Through Movement*, Macdonald &
Evans, 1971, and M. North, 'An Investigation into Movement
Characteristics of Children of Various Ability', M.Ed. thesis,
Leicester University, 1969. There are also films: *Looking at Children*,
Series 1, 2 and 3 (IE Films Ltd, 2 South Audley Street, London W1).

technique. Examples are given in the next chapter of student's work, indicating the kind of level that can be expected after a relatively short time.

Does one person's movement affect or influence that of another?

Effort 'contamination' is an expression used to indicate how effort quality can be 'picked up' by one person from another. It is a very subtle movement pattern to observe, yet it is well known in everyday life. For instance, a teacher has an effect upon a class because of his personal qualities, many of which are revealed in his movement patterns. To some degree, a knowledge of this phenomenon can be used by a teacher who has learned to differentiate movement qualities; though all good teachers and leaders know that quietness and calm engender a similar response and that excitement is 'infectious'. This phenomenon explains some of the experiences we all have, of changes in our own moods and feelings when we join different groups, or meet people. There are those who always seem to 'infect' others with their depression and gloom, or to inspire with their gaiety and optimism. At a more intimate level, it relates to the capacity one human being has to 'feel' with, or understand, the emotions and feelings of another person.

Laban's influence on the study of movement characteristics

Although human movement was studied in ancient times in great detail (especially in China, where remnants of the system have been sketchily preserved) and knowledge of movement has been used for religious, cultural and therapeutic purposes in most societies, comparatively little is known about the language of movement in our own culture outside the specialist field of movement practitioners. Today, in the West, we owe our greatest debt to one man, Laban, who had the vision to initiate movement study at the depth which we are now exploring and charting. Laban was an East European, born in Bratislava, whose love of drama, theatre, dance, architecture and mathematics led him to study people and relate his varied interests to the psychology of human beings. He was a contemporary of Jung, and although their spheres of investigation and original ideas are seemingly distant, he realised that the study of human movement would provide a means for the greater understanding of man and his complicated psychology.

From the beginning, Laban recognised that no description of movement which excluded either the developing process and sequence of action, or the qualitative (non-measurable) aspects of movement, could possibly give any real understanding of the inner workings of the human being. His discoveries were not inventions, but the recognition of laws and fundamental patterns available for us all to see, but closed from us until his original approach opened our eyes to the 'content' of movement. Laban described the qualitative aspects of movement ('effort' was his chosen term for the inner impulse to movement which gives colour and texture to our actions) and the spatial aspects, for which he developed a theory of space harmony comparable with musical harmony.

His work involved artistic creation in drama, mime and dance, and he also worked with the mentally and physically handicapped. His knowledge was used in industry and commerce for the selection and training of personnel and for vocational guidance, and he stimulated others to apply some of his ideas to education. Throughout his life, Laban's awareness of people and their movement, and their relationships and situations in life, inspired him to an increasing refinement of his theories. He published very little, although there are many unpublished papers. Most of his work was passed on directly to the few pupils he could find who would and could go deeply enough into movement study to follow him. He never 'researched' himself in the accepted sense; in fact, he made few claims to detailed application of his ideas. This is left for others to do as his ideas gradually become clarified and brought to workable dimensions.

The development of detailed movement study in this country owes its source to Laban's work, although many of the descriptions of movement will not be found in his writings because they have been developed and understood only since his death, and knowledge and experience drawn from other investigators as well as from other fields of research have been incorporated.

Laban left invaluable tools for research in his notation systems, which reflected his new approach to the study of movement. The notation has been omitted in this book, but for reference see *Personality Assessment through Movement.*

Many investigators have developed systems and categories of movements based on quantitative and measurable aspects. No one except Laban has analysed and notated *qualitative* movement sequences and processes.

The system used here to differentiate movement aspects is essentially that discovered originally by Laban, but developed since his death into a more systematic form. A great deal of further research needs to be undertaken to provide information which can be used to deepen our knowledge.

Four aspects of movement

In the examples of observations of children given later, it will be seen that the following four aspects of movement are clearly defined, although interrelated:[2]

    (a) The body—what moves;
    (b) The quality or 'effort'—how the body moves;
    (c) The space—where the body moves;
    (d) Relationships—with what or whom the body moves.

These aspects will take up the next four main sections of this chapter.

(A) THE BODY

Those aspects which may be observed, notated and considered include:

Inwards and outwards flow   The flow of movement in the body can be inwards towards the centre of the body, or outwards towards the extremities.

Narrow and wide use of the body   Although there is a strong connection between the inward body flow and narrowness in the body, and between outward flow and the wide use of the body, occasionally the opposite is found. For instance, a nine-year-old boy who used both narrow and wide body action, had only clear outward flow and almost totally lacked inward flow.

[2] There are detailed descriptions of the terms used throughout this chapter in *Personality Assessment through Movement.*

Body awareness This is recognisable, and can be described as 'knowing' (though not necessarily consciously) where the body is, what part is moving, and the various complicated relationships of one part of the body to another. It implies an ability to 'envisage' or 'feel' its shape and form, as well as its size and action.

Unity of the upper and lower parts of the body Sometimes a human body moves as if it were working in two separate halves, the expression or action in the lower half being disconnected from the upper half.

Unity of the centre of the body and the extremities Again, some children have good connections between the body centre and the limbs, others inititate action and relate it to the limbs only without a central link.[3] Other 'splits' in the body occur, although the two mentioned are perhaps the most commonly encountered in primary-school children; for example, splits between the right and left sides of the body (literally, the right side not 'knowing what the left is doing) or between head and trunk, and so on.

Trunk movements initiated in different parts Movements can come from the centre of levity (roughly located in the upper-trunk area), the body centre, and the centre of gravity (roughly located in the lower-trunk area). For example, movements which are habitually initiated from, or involve, the centre of gravity, differ in kind and expression from those involving mainly the centre of levity. Children vary in the use of their bodies: in a study of twenty-eight children, only four were equally proficient in the use of all three areas; even so, one or other area was noted in each child as being more characteristically used. The child with centre-of-gravity tends to be more 'earthbound' and dynamic, while the child with centre-of-levity is more buoyant, upward-reaching and lighter. These differences have nothing to do with the actual body build or shape of the body, for a fat child can move actively from the centre of levity, and a small bony child can move from the centre of gravity.

Symmetry and asymmetry of the body These body 'pref-

[3] An example can be seen of this in the film of two one-year-old babies, *Series III, i, Jeremy and Anthony, aged one*; also in the film *Gerald and Frank, Series I, i* (IE Films Ltd).

erences' are seen in both movement, and in bodily attitudes or positions. Either the whole body shows these attributes or perhaps only the upper or lower halves, or even the head.

Shapes of the body One can observe various aspects of body shape:

1 The ability to make clear shapes and positions (note that this has a close link with body awareness);
2 Round body shapes (like a ball);
3 Flat body shapes (like a wall);
4 Elongated body shapes (like an arrow or pin);
5 Twisted body shapes (like a spiky or twisted wire).

Numbers (2) to (5) are the four basic shapes which a body can assume. Often they appear combined; for instance, an elongated twist, or a twisted upper body on a spread-out lower half. Some people can change from one to another with ease (in the study of twenty-eight children, two could do this) but most people have a more limited range, excluding one or more; even if their range is wider, they give preference to one or other. Of the children studied, a few showed little awareness of their body shape—they had 'no body'. For instance, one child lacked all but an infrequent use of twisted shapes, another used rounded and flat shapes exclusively, and another, while using all four, used the flat, two-dimensional shape less frequently.

Manual dexterity The skilful handling of material and objects, the use of the fingers in fine manipulations or whole hand/body in grosser movement.

The above are broad divisions, and indicate some differentiations in the use of the body. Typical and characteristic use of the body by the child can be recognised when many observations are made and recorded, each movement phrase or position being noted as it occurs, and the records analysed later. An observant teacher who is with a class frequently will know these characteristics and, because of this knowledge, will have a fairly good idea of children's responses.

(B) EFFORT

'Effort' is the term used to refer to the inner urge or drive towards movement. The resulting movement will be either an action (a gesture, step, body shift, working action) if fully developed, or, in one initiated which then dies away, a 'shadow movement' (a small body movement seemingly with no external aim—a raised eyebrow or frown, a tapping finger, a shoulder twitch, a fleeting look of recognition). Usually, an action is preceded by a shadow movement, or sequence of shadow movements which become enlarged and lead towards the ultimate action. In this phrase or sequence or series of movements, a whole 'story' of inner meaning can be discerned by understanding the particular sequence of movement elements. It is, therefore, essential to be able to observe and notate exactly what a sequence of elements is, and how it appears in the body.

Sometimes movements appear which show a contradiction, not only between speech and body movements, but between movements of the body and 'shadow' movements. This split is more or less serious according to the situation and frequency of its appearance. 'Playing a part' or 'putting on an act' often leads to this discrepancy.

Phrases

Phrases (sentences and sequences) are of paramount importance in personality assessment; each individual has his own 'chosen' patterns. Many people have a great number of different kinds of phrases, or sentences, of movement which are typical for them, others have a smaller number. The length of phrase or sentence also varies according to function and personality. Some people have available for use long and complex 'sentences' when appropriate, others have only 'simple' sentences. This, as in the development of verbal language, appears to relate to maturity.

From the notated sequences or phrases, it has been possible to estimate whether the transitions between one movement quality and the next are generally good (appropriate), or jerky. When and in what circumstances they appear so, is seen from the movement phrases.

Rhythmical abilities   These can be observed where there is good alternation between elements of time and weight and when phrases appear frequently in which an innate rhythmical sense is apparent.

Mechanical or metrical movement This is even, non-stressed repetitiveness.

Resiliency There is an inner 'rebound' or resilience, which is shown in phrases of rebound alternations—a strong movement usually rebounds into a lighter one—and 'bounciness'.

Immediate reactions These are observable where a movement phrase occurs without a pause, or 'held' position, at the beginning.

Delayed reactions These occur where a pause or a held position, precedes the movement phrase.

Crescendo phrases These are phrases which build up in intensity of dynamic or time.

Decrescendo phrases These decrease or die away after an initial burst of energy. Both the crescendo and decrescendo phrases incorporate a large number of variations of increase and decrease, that is, in intensity, force, time, and flow, and in all combinations of these.

The elements of movement

The elements of movement, which are like the letters or sounds of the written or spoken language, can be described in simple categories; though, in fact, they appear in movement always in combination with each other within the sequences described above and only very rarely as isolated elements. Just as a letter or sound in isolation has little meaning, so an isolated movement element has only a limited interest; but how it is combined with other elements when it appears within a phrase is significant.

The single elements of movement may be described in relation to a person as being his inner attitude[4] towards:

1 the weight of his body;
2 time, that is, his subjective or personal experience of time, not the measurable length;
3 the flow of movement in his body;
4 space, that is, his bodily attitude of directness or flexibility, which reflects mental directness or flexibility; and not the shapes or directions of his movement.

[4] The word 'attitude' is used here attempts to differentiate between an actual measurable, or quantitative, use of body weight, time and so on, and a subjective qualitative aspect. It is the latter qualitative aspect which is being discussed.

1 *A person's attitude towards the weight of his body* An individual can use his weight with sensitivity, or with forcefulness, or he can weakly indulge in a 'state of heaviness'. These, then, are the broad categories, but they are modified in degrees. It is only possible to describe a quality in quantitative terms as 'more or less sensitive', and so on.

To illustrate two opposite extremes of attitude which can be observed, a line is used, the middle of which denotes the moment of change from one attitude to another:

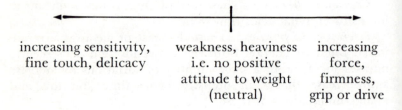

| increasing sensitivity, fine touch, delicacy | weakness, heaviness i.e. no positive attitude to weight (neutral) | increasing force, firmness, grip or drive |

The above consideration of movement is directly connected with sensation, but, because of the way that this is mixed with and a part of other elements, generalised statements about it are difficult to make without numerous qualifications. However, any combination of movement elements which includes weight can be reckoned to have association with bodily sensations. It is perhaps the most developed element at birth. A newborn infant, and even the unborn child, shows a developed firmness and grip, and to a lesser degree but certainly to some extent, sensitivity and fineness of touch.

Every baby exhibits quite different qualities and rhythms in its movement patterns, some being obviously sensitive and 'light', in comparison with those who are forceful and energetic. Babies' reactions to touch are also markedly different: that which for one baby is a comforting 'rollicking' firmness and energy in holding, can be for another intrusive and disturbing. A sensitive mother knows how differently she must handle each one of her children and how differently each responds, even in relation only to this element of movement. The same, in fact, applies to the other three aspects of effort, and indicates that many basic attitudes and movement patterns are present at birth. Each child responds differently and needs different handling from a mother; indeed, the same mother can respond quite differently to different children. These inter-related patterns between baby and mother will surely throw some light upon the autistic child, for the kind of handling and caring which will suit one baby, may be inadequate for another and cause him to withdraw.

2 *A person's attitude towards time*   An individual experiences time subjectively and characteristically, sometimes differently on different occasions. He may experience urgency, liveliness and excitability (almost 'vibrational' or trembling in frequent repetition) or their opposites of leisureliness and lingering sustainment of attitude. Again, a line can be drawn to illustrate these extremes.

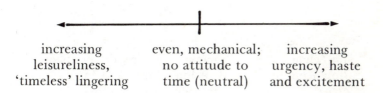

increasing	even, mechanical;	increasing
leisureliness,	no attitude to	urgency, haste
'timeless' lingering	time (neutral)	and excitement

This element of movement is connected with decisiveness, the capacity for intuitive leaps, hesitation, delayed action, excitability and so on. Some aspects of the time element are discernible in newborn babies; for instance, in their excitability or placidity, and in their basic reactions to stimuli. This element, however, is perhaps less differentiated than that of weight, and becomes more clearly defined as an 'attitude' only after the first weeks or months. Nevertheless, it is observable and clearly different as between one infant and another; some babies show an immediate vitality, and rhythmical alternations are seen from birth; others have a more even 'unliveliness'. This element, then, is clearly a part of basic personal rhythm. For example, rhythms of infants' crying (their means of vocalising the body rhythms) have individual differences which are very familiar to mothers and nurses.

In describing rhythm, we are, of course, involving the previously described element of weight (the attitude towards the weight of the body). Phrases appear where the two are combined, as in repeated, light, urgent movements (or sounds) increasing to strong, elongated movements or sounds, which gradually fade.

3 *A person's attitude towards the flow of movement* An individual's attitude towards the flow of movement may be free, uninhibited and easy, or it may be restrained, inhibited and controlled. To illustrate these extremes a line may be drawn:

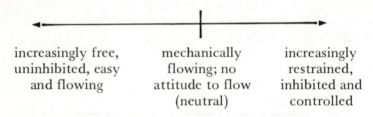

| increasingly free, uninhibited, easy and flowing | mechanically flowing; no attitude to flow (neutral) | increasingly restrained, inhibited and controlled |

This element of movement is directly connected with emotional inhibition or freedom. Infants at birth show these extremes quite clearly, in tightly held movements and in flowing ones (closely connected with breathing) and this element is often combined in infants with their attitude to the weight of the body. As its most obvious, strength and grip are associated with bound flow, while sensitivity is associated with ease of flow. Inner moods or attitudes can change quickly from light/free to strong/bound, sometimes interspersed with time elements. An example of this is a movement phrase which starts sensitively with free flow, gradually becomes less free, changing to repeated (agitated) sudden movements with a bound flow, and finally bringing strength into hitting and thrashing actions.

4 *A person's attitude towards space* An individual's bodily attitudes of directness or flexibility reflect the same qualities in his mind. For example, embarrassed avoidance might reveal itself in one individual in a movement of 'direct'

seizing up (direct bound flow with strength) and in another person in a flexible twisting away from the focus (flexible, bound and strong). A line shows the extremes:

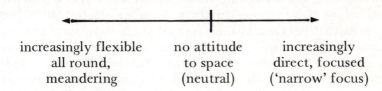

| increasingly flexible all round, meandering | no attitude to space (neutral) | increasingly direct, focused ('narrow' focus) |

This element rarely appears in a positive way in newborn infants, but is noticeable in bodily reactions, as in, say, twisting and wringing in discomfort, or in the direct stretching of the body. As development proceeds, it becomes gradually differentiated as a true 'attitude' in a positive sense; that is, it relates to a focus. Probably one of the earliest manifestations of directness is in the eye contact of the baby with the mother. It is interesting that, as our research progresses, we occasionally find a baby of a few days old who can already focus, and whose eyes follow a moving object.[5]

This element of movement is directly connected with organisation and cognitive processes. It therefore seems reasonable to suppose that it is the latest to be differentiated in babies.

Summary of the elements of movement

To summarise, the elements of movement can be recognised as the person's attitude towards:

1	weight	firmness and grip	or	fine touch, sensitivity
2	time	sustained leisureliness	or	urgency, agitation
3	space	flexibility and 'all-roundness'	or	directed focus

[5] Ongoing research with newborn babies by M. North and T. Newman, directed by Dr M.D. Marshak, University of London Institute of Education.

4   flow   free   *or*   bound,
                uninhibited   restrained

In making a movement 'portrait', the presence of the above-mentioned elements alone would not reveal much, for all of us have access to them to some degree. It is the particular frequency of their appearance in movement phrases and the degrees which are used that are really significant, as well as the other elements together with which each is used. For instance, one of the children out of the sample of twenty-eight, mentioned earlier, had access to all elements, but lightness, suddenness, directness and free flow were characteristically used more frequently than the other elements; another child had a weaker pattern, by showing only strength, free flow and bound flow (stressing bound flow) as actively used, with lightness, suddenness, sustainment and directness being rarely used—perhaps latent qualities, not fully developed. Flexibility was used so infrequently as to be virtually unavailable.

Ability to alternate between opposite attitudes

Some people show the ability to alternate between opposite attitudes to each factor as required, moving between

> sensitivity and firmness;
> leisureliness and urgency;
> flexibility and directness;
> free and bound flow.

A capacity for alternation shows a developed use of elements, which by no means everyone acquires.

Combinations of three elements appearing at the same time

There are various combinations of three of the elements together. All four elements, with equal stress, rarely appear in a movement, but the three-element combination appears in what Laban refers to as 'externalised drives'.

There are four groups of externalised drives, each having its own characteristic: the 'flowless'; the 'timeless'; the 'spaceless'; and the 'weightless'.

There are eight variations of the weight—time—space combination (that is, 'flowless'). This combination of elements characterises practical action, whether directed towards external objects or towards thoughts and ideas. An individual in whom this group of elements predominates will be essentially practical, down-to-earth and realistic, although these tendencies will obviously be modified by whatever associated movement patterns he has.

To describe the eight basic variations in words can be misleading, because there are so many subtle distinctions and stresses within each one. Provided the words are used only in an attempt to communicate the general differences, however, the direct movement notation will describe to a trained observer the implications inherent in each.

1   Firm, sudden, direct (a hitting, thrusting action);
2   Sensitive, sustained, flexible (a floating action);
3   Firm, sustained, direct (a pressing action);
4   Sensitive, sudden, flexible (a flicking action);
5   Firm, sudden, flexible (a slashing action);
6   Sensitive, sustained, direct (a gliding action);
7   Firm, sustained, flexible (a wringing action);
8   Sensitive, sudden, direct (a dabbing action).

Apart from increases or decreases in the degree to which each element is present, each combination might have one or two elements stressed at the expense of the rest. This might give very different interpretations.

For instance, a thrust, which is strong, sudden and directed, becomes

(a)   a piercing, penetrating thrust if the directness is stressed;
(b)   a jabbing, urgent thrust if the suddenness is stressed;
(c)   a crushing, forceful thrust if the strength is stressed.

Similarly, there are eight variations of each of the other three combinations of movement:

weight, time, flow (spaceless)
weight, space, flow (timeless)
space, time, flow (weightless).

Weight, time and flow combinations lack the qualitative space elements and characterise what, for want of a better term, can be described as a 'feeling' action. This can be understood if it is recognised that the element of space (the thinking, rational element) is absent, and the element of flow (which is related to feeling and emotion) is incorporated.

Weight, space and flow combinations lack the qualitative time elements: they are 'out of time' or 'timeless' and characterise a 'spell-like' action, exerting a kind of hypnotic influence, such as direct, strong, bound movement, or a sensitive, free flexibility (like being absorbed in weaving a dress or a fantasy story).

Space, time and flow combinations lack the bodily sensation or the weight element, and might be loosely described as 'envisaging' action. Just as we noted earlier that the weight element is the most firmly established of the four in babies, so this combination, lacking weight, is observed to be the last of these 'externalised drives' to be developed.

Combination of two elements appearing at the same time

When an element appears in conjunction with another, it is, in a sense, no longer the same element, but something new. For example, the colours red and blue, when mixed, appear together as purple, a colour in its own right. Two elements thus fused appear most frequently in our movement. When one element is stressed at the expense of the other, the 'colour' will change (just as purple can become a 'bluish purple' or a 'reddish purple', with many possible shades in between). There are six ways in which two elements at a time can be combined:

1 *Flow/time combinations* typify 'mobility', changeability, flux and adaptation in various ways:

> bound/sudden
> free/sustained
> bound/sustained
> free/sudden.

The inner attitude of mental mobility can be a positive, lively attribute within its 'normal' dimensions. If exaggerated, it can be flighty, restless and changeable; and, if unbalanced by other capacities, it will show an unease or 'lack of concentration'.

2 *Weight/flow combinations* typify unconscious attitudes of sensation and feeling, which lack space and time alertness:

> firm/bound
> sensitive/free
> firm/free
> sensitive/bound.

All creative people seem to be well endowed with these combinations and use them positively. If such combinations become exaggerated, they become less positive, as in bound flow and strength (where they can be revelations of a sort of nightmarish cramp) or in free flow and lightness (a revelation of vague meandering in a kind of daydream).

3 *Weight/time combinations* typify the warm, rhythmical and earthy attitudes:

> firm/sudden
> sensitive/sustained
> firm/sustained
> sensitive/sudden.

When exaggerated, such 'earthy' attitudes can become brutal, as in exaggerated strength and urgency, or strength and sustainment.

4 *Weight/space combinations* are the opposite of time/ flow. These are the stable, solid and reliable, unchanging attitudes, though if exaggerated they may become essentially static and stubborn, as in exaggerated strength and directness:

> strong/direct
> sensitive/flexible
> strong/flexible
> sensitive/direct.

5 *Time/space combinations* are the opposite of weight/ flow. These are the attitudes which are alert, externally aware and practical:

> direct/sudden
> flexible/direct
> direct/sustained
> flexible/sudden.

6 *Space/flow combinations* are the opposite of weight/ time and typify cool, abstract and remote attitudes:

> direct/bound
> flexible/free
> flexible/bound
> direct/free.

Actual observations made of the behaviour of children (or adults) are never as neat as these summaries imply. All kinds of degrees (lessened or exaggerated) or preferred elements, modify the movement and preclude any automatic application of these 'interpretations'. Many words have been put in inverted commas because they represent only some kind of approximation to the real meanings of these signs—which have far greater subtleties than there are words to illustrate them. Most of the descriptive words used in everyday language suggest a combination of many elements, the mixture of many movement aspects; they are therefore very inexact.

(C) SPATIAL DIRECTIONS AND PATTERNS

Various aspects which may be observed and notated:

Shaping gestures

1   General ability to shape clearly and precisely (i.e., the ability of the person to 'shape' his environment);
2   Large shapes;
3   Small shapes;
4   Complex shapes;
5   Simple shapes.

These categories simplify the very detailed observation of shapes (angular, round or twisted) and their particular orientation in the space around the person, that is, in his personal sphere.

Placement of shapes

1   Far (at, or going towards, full extension of the body); or
2   Near to the body.

The use of the usual intermediate space is assumed, as it is the 'normal' for everyday life.

Planes of movement

Often an individual has a tendency to use one plane more frequently than the other two planes, although some people use all three frequently, with perhaps only slightly less use of one than of the other two.

The vertical plane stresses the up-and-down dimension. The horizontal plane stresses the side-to-side movements, parallel to the earth, opening, spreading, communicating to others at the same level, with an ease of turning and taking in wide areas. The sagittal plane stresses the forward and backward directions, advancing and withdrawing, folding in, or travelling forwards.

Levels of space which are used by an individual

High level: the movement tends to be initiated by the centre of levity and leads towards resilience, rebound (as in a high, 'bouncy' walker).
Medium level: the movement is not stressed towards high or low, but has a 'swingy' (waltz-like) quality.
Deep level: downward stress of movement which tends to be impactive, firm and 'down to earth', usually associated with the use of the centre of gravity.

(D) RELATIONSHIPS

Relationships between the moving person and objects or with other people are noted in association with the particular movement which is being observed. Subtle observations of how one child responds to another, will mean watching the timing and placement and bodily use (details of which are indicated above). Many observed movement-patterns relate to the person's own relationships with himself, and with his different (sometimes conflicting) attitudes.

This section appears to present a formidable list of movement aspects, but in fact in a general way they are all familiar and simple to observe. In the training of students, it has been found that it is only necessary to draw attention to different movement aspects and clarify what has been observed intuitively already. Accurate observation can be developed best by practice. In order to assist practice, a series of films on the movement of junior-school children has been made[6] and the accompanying notes to these films will be of value to the teacher and student. The examples in the next chapter are taken from the work of students in teacher training at Sidney Webb College, London. They illustrate the beginnings of observation training. Examples of more advanced 'movement portraits' can be seen in *Personality Assessment through Movement.*

[6] Series I, i, ii, iii, and Series II, i, ii, iii: six ten-minute films, black and white, sound. Obtainable from IE Films Ltd.

13 Movement Assessments of Junior-School Children: Examples of Students' Work

MARY: AGED SEVEN

Introduction

Mary is a slightly built, dark-haired girl of seven years who, at our first meeting, chatted to me easily and fluently. When getting ready for the movement session she undressed quickly and efficiently and, because she was ready first, helped her friend to hang up her clothes. My first impression was that of a lively, energetic child who appeared reasonably confident.

During the movement session, however, I noticed that Mary kept close to her friend Suzannah, and both children remained on the edge of the class, any travelling being done in a fairly restricted area of the room. It was also noticeable that Mary rarely performed any movement the first time the class was asked, but joined in at the second attempt. Her first attempt at any movement tended to be almost a shadow movement and in many cases this was mainly in the arms rather than in the body. Mary also made constant quick darting looks around the class during the movement sessions as if seeking reassurance that what she was doing conformed to the rest of the children's movements.

During the different sessions I spent with Mary it became obvious that, while she used a reasonably wide range of movement when stimulated by tangible objects, such as clay or paint, in movement sessions where her body was the instrument for creativity and communication her response was very limited. Although it must be remembered that Mary was used to working with such items as clay and paint, and was unused to movement sessions, the question could still be asked whether this lack of bodily response shows a basic insecurity in her as a person.

Body aspects

Mary's body shape is mainly narrow and pin-like and is often symmetrical. In many instances, she showed her inclination to retain a closed body attitude rather than an open one. The first indication of this was noted in a tendency to stand with her toes pointed slightly inwards. It also showed on several occasions when she crouched down to the floor and, although her legs were splayed out, the legs above the knees were kept closely pressed together. A further instance was where wide positions were asked for, when Mary stretched her arms widely open but kept her fingers slightly curled and also did not extend her legs as fully as possible. With encouragement, however, Mary would adopt a really open position, as I found when I worked with her and two other children for a short session away from the rest of the class, but in the next movement session Mary reverted to her previous position.

It was also apparent that Mary was much more aware of the upper part of her body and her movements were mainly initiated from the shoulder and chest areas. When the children were asked during a movement session to travel round the room using each step to bring their knees up as high as possible, Mary bent the upper part of her body down towards her knees rather than bringing her knees up towards her body. There appeared strong indications that Mary lacks a body centre, causing a split upper/lower level. What does this imply? Is there the possibility that Mary will tend to operate on a surface level, lacking a solid base, and are there any psychological implications in her tendency to retain a closed rather than an open body position?

When running and jumping, Mary tended to take off on the left foot and often, though not always, turned to the left. Although she used her right hand for writing, drawing, and so on, she often used her left hand to pick up objects or to take something from another person. Again during the movement sessions, when asked, for instance, to step and put one hand on the floor, Mary used her left hand, and when asked to balance on one hand and foot she chose the left hand and right foot. During this particular activity she always placed her hand behind her body and balanced in this position rather than placing her hand on the ground in front of her body, unlike the majority of the children in the class.

Effort

The most outstanding and noticeable of Mary's effort qualities was that of fine touch. During a movement session, when asked to take 'big strong steps, like a giant', she took reasonably large strides but the quality remained light; also, when she was asked to imagine that she was pulling along a large animal, she achieved a certain amount of strength in her hands and arms but nowhere else in her body. When pretending to lift a heavy object from the floor, the weight element was almist non-existent and the entire movement was rather 'distant' in quality, being sustained, direct and bound. Her phrasing in this instance was slightly impulsive and, as with most of her phrases, faded away at the end.

Having observed this almost complete lack of strength during the movement session, it was interesting to watch Mary working with clay—the activity chosen after the movement session. Although her initial approach to the material was somewhat tentative, because, to use her own words 'It feels all messy and sticky', after a short while she started to use really strong movements to pound and punch the clay to make it workable. Initially, this strength was mainly in her hands and arms, but as she become more engrossed in the effort to prepare the clay, she stood up from the chair and used her body as well as her hands.

Her fine touch returned as she started to model a head of a character from *The Lion, the Witch and the Wardrobe*, which she informed me was the story her teacher was reading to them.

Conclusion

Body shape: mainly pin-like and symmetrical.

Main effort qualities used:
1   light/direct/sustained
2   light/flexible/free (hands and arms only)
3   light/bound/neutral space.

Typical phrasing:
1 light/direct/sustained changing to heavy/direct/sustained (i.e. a weakening phrase)
2 light/free/sustained changing to light/bound/neutral space and held.

Body attitude: tends towards a closed rather than open position.

Space: Gestures mainly kept close to the body. Prefers to move medium/high rather than at lower level. Keeps to edge of room. Travels mainly in straight pathways, sometimes circular. (In her drawings, however, Mary used the three basic shapes, circular, twisted figure-of-eight, and angular.)

Relationship with other children and adults: Friendly with members of class, but having one particular friend with whom she stayed during all of the sessions. (At one point, when the children were asked to change partners, Mary changed for a moment but then managed to return to her own particular friend.) Seemed reasonably at ease when meeting other students at college for first time.

Response to different materials

As already stated, although Mary showed little or not strength during the movement sessions, when working with clay this particular response become apparent and was present in the body as well as the hands and arms.

When given gummed paper to cut into shapes for a picture, Mary chose to cut quite a number of angular shapes, after which she arranged some of them to form a house, discarding those which she did not want to use.

Her response to finger painting surprised me, as there was no hesitation (as there had been in her initial response to clay). Perhaps this was due to the fact that she feels completely at home with paint, or perhaps because it is possible to do finger painting without getting the entire hand covered with paint. It was interesting to note how she started to make the pattern from the blob of thickened paint placed in the centre of the paper, going back to the centre each time to gather up enough paint for the next section.

Mary then continued with circular and flexible-type movements, gradually bringing in two more fingers (the initial pattern was made using the forefinger only) and the original pattern was replaced.

Space

When Mary was asked to move around the room freely in different directions, and to use as much of the space as possible, she remained in a fairly restricted area and kept to the edge of the room. This pattern of behaviour remained when I worked with Mary, together with three other children, alone. Although, in this instance, she travelled completely round the room area she still never went to the centre unless specifically told to do so. What might this imply?

Mary's gestures are nearly always close to the body, rather angular and small. Her arms are rarely flung wide, or open, even when running and leaping. Also, when running and jumping, she tended to bend her body up when in the air.

When engaging in rising and sinking movements on the spot, Mary went mainly from low to reasonably high, very rapidly. When asked to travel sometimes high and sometimes low, she mainly travelled with arms high, although not stretching upwards in her body, and with eyes focusing downwards rather than upwards. I never saw her travel on the floor as a number of the other children did.

Mary uses a mixture of direct and flexible movements although flexibility is more apparent in her arms, hands and fingers than in her body. For example, when the class was asked to use flexible, twisting movements to rise up from a low position on the floor, Mary used a direct movement to bring her body up, but made flexible twisted shapes with her hands and arms. The same pattern was used when moving from high to low. Whether this inflexibility of body is due to an inner attitude of inflexibility or whether it is due to lack of opportunity or encouragement to use her body flexibly is yet another question which arises.

The type of movement which Mary seemed most responsive to in the movement sessions, was when asked to pretend she was creeping towards something frightening. This she did with real sensitivity, using fine touch, free flow and sustainment at the beginning of each short phrase of movement, and this changed to a bound, held movement at the end.

This, then, was the only type of movement where Mary held her position at the end of each phrase; normally, her phrases faded out at the end.

Although in situations where she was handling tangible objects and in situations outside the movement sessions, Mary used a mixture of sudden and sustained movements, within the movement sessions she seemed more at ease with sustained movements, and in many cases there was a 'timeless' quality present. There was a tendency to make light and sudden shadow movements with her hands and she often touched her face with her hands.

PENNY AND JEAN: TWINS, AGED TWELVE PLUS

General background
Penny and Jean were admitted to a special school (educationally sub-normal) in 1970. Prior to this, they had both attended a residential school for delicate children at Hayling Island. While the children were at the residential school, the parents never visited them and wrote on an average of only once a term. Although this gives an impression of a lack of care, it is necessary to remember that lack of money may have prevented them from travelling to Hayling Island, and as they themselves were of limited intelligence, letter-writing was probably too laborious to be undertaken frequently. There are five other children in the family.

While there is a close bond between the two children, who are never far apart, and will defend each other against other members of the class, this does not prevent them from having quite fierce fights with each other occasionally.

The children are both well-behaved in class and appear to have no major social or emotional problems. Jean is more shy than Penny and finds conversation more difficult.

Although the twins are almost identical in appearance, it is interesting to note that their body carriage and movement is, in some instances, quite different. It is for this reason that I have discussed the children together in order to draw comparisons between them.

Body aspects

After a few visits to the school, I found that I could tell the twins apart, even from a distance, because of the differences in the way they moved.

Penny has a more open body attitude than Jean, who tends to be more closed in and withdrawn. This attitude is linked with the fact that Jean is the slightly more withdrawn and shy of the two children. In walking and running, Penny moves more lightly and freely than Jean. Jean walks and runs with the upper part of her body bent slightly forward, and with arms hanging limply, giving an appearance of withdrawal from the centre of the body. Moreover, there is a tendency for Jean to use one section of her body in isolation. For example, when throwing a ball, she uses her hand and arm, but the rest of her body remains passive. Penny, on the other hand, involves her entire body to a much greater extent. In this respect, Jean appears to have less body awareness than Penny.

Both girls have a tendency to be symmetrical, although Jean frequently sits, having her upper body symmetrical and her lower body asymmetrical. Both of them prefer to move near the ground. When working on fixed apparatus, neither girl likes climbing but both enjoy rolling on the mat. If asked to climb a wall bar, Penny will climb more easily than Jean, who generally will only venture up about three rungs and then climbs down.

Effort

Although, when walking, running and so on, Jean uses mainly bound flow with weight and Penny uses lighter and less bound qualities, this situation is almost reversed when the girls are working with their hands. The first time I noticed this was when the twins were both drawing and Penny used her pencil with such force that she made holes in the paper at several points (the action was exaggerated strength with bound flow, increasing to cramp). This tendency showed in all activities when using hands. Even when building with 'Leggo' or other construction sets, Penny grasped the pieces rather firmly and was less adept at putting them together than Jean, who used a light touch, often using just the tips of her fingers.

It seems that these different qualities, used in different situations, reflect the basically dissimilar attitude of the twins to what they are doing. For example, Jean appears to be happier when working with her hands, while Penny prefers running, skipping and jumping. This also seems to be so during movement sessions, when Penny enjoys moving freely about the room but Jean prefers to stay more or less in one position and prefers arm gestures to bodily movement. This again points to her limited body awareness.

If Jean is at all worried or concerned, she often clasps her hands together with a great deal of strong, bound-flow tension and flexibility. This was noticeable on many occasions, one of them at the swimming pool when Jean could not bring herself to get into the water despite encouragement from the teacher, her sister and me. Another occasion when this was apparent was at the beginning of movement sessions, when Jean obviously felt rather strange and inhibited.

When cutting shapes from gummed paper, Penny used a constant shape and pattern until she had completed the design, but Jean changed halfway through. This consistency is a feature of Penny's who is also very critical of her own work. When drawing and painting, she will often destroy the work before it is completed, but then restarts the same piece of work. It seems, therefore, that her bound flow and weight and general air of tension when working with her hands may be due, not to her dislike of the actual activitiy, but to her awareness that she will probably experience dissatisfaction with the end result.

Jean's movements are mainly phrased impactively, although on occasions they are impulsive. Penny moves in rather even phrases mainly, but when working with her hands there is a tendency towards impactive movement.

Both Penny and Jean will tap their feet when singing or listening to music, although it is usually Penny who starts first, Jean following after a short while. Many shadow movements of the face can be observed in both children and these movements are of a light, sudden nature, often repeated.

Space

Penny moves more directly than Jean, who is slightly more

flexible, although this flexibility is more apparent in her hands and arms than in her body (and again when working with materials). It is as if, given the stimulus of different materials, she can experience, at least with her hands, a different quality of movement from that normally experienced within her body.

Jean also seems to prefer to move within her own kinesphere.[1] She will stretch up and out and make fairly large sweeping gestures, but she usually does this without moving into a new space in the room. Penny, on the other hand, will move quite freely about the room, but nearly always move in a direct pathway.

When the girls were on the floor during a movement session, curling up in different ways, Penny would curl her body, but Jean kept her head and her back straight on the floor, although she bent her knees up to her body.

Neither of the girls uses gestures a great deal in everyday movement, but when they do, they both tend to confine them to fairly small movements which in general follow an inwards direction.

It would seem that Jean is in some ways less happy in space than Penny. If, perhaps, as previously suggested, Jean is less secure in herself as a person, it is more difficult for her to be aware of the space around and her relationship to it.

Relationships

As already mentioned, there is a fairly close bond between the twins and although, on occasion, they have a tendency to fight, they spend a lot of time together. Perhaps they are in many ways dependent on each other for a reasonably stable relationship; however, this does not mean that they exclude other people, as they are quite friendly, Penny is able to establish a relationship with another person rather more easily than Jean. For example, when I first started to visit the school, Penny talked to me fairly easily during the first visit, but it was only after a few visits that Jean would chat easily or approach me of her own accord. Penny will also move away from her own table to be with another group; Jean rarely does this.

[1] The space around a person.

There appears little doubt that, of the two, Penny has more confidence. At the swimming pool, for example, Penny was quite confident, and although she was unable to swim, she was holding on to the rail and kicking out with her feet, whereas Jean was unable even to get into the water. Both girls had visited the pool previously and there is no pressure on any of the children to attend the swimming sessions. Although Jean says she wants to learn to swim, I wonder if, in fact, she goes simply to be with Penny?

When talking to adults, Jean has a habit of looking away most of the time, only occasionally glancing at the person to whom she is talking. It is as if she is communicating with them verbally, but withdrawing at the same time. This tendency lessens as she knows the person better, but is still present to some degree.

ANDREW: AGED TWELVE PLUS

General background

Andrew is the fourth child in a family of six. In appearance he is a healthy, well-cared-for child, and well-built for his age. His mother was in contact with a case of Rubella at approximately the sixth week of her pregnancy. Andrew appeared quite normal at birth, and he followed a normal pattern of development, apart from his lack of verbal communication, which did not begin until he was three years of age and stopped after only a few months.

He started school at five years of age but was retained for only two months, during which time he was referred to the educational psychologist and diagnosed as being mentally retarded with psychotic tendencies. He was regarded as being uneducable and was recommended for admission to a junior training centre. This decision was resisted by the parents and the Ministry of Education upheld the parents' opinion.

Andrew was eventually admitted on a part-time basis to an infant school. While this is an ordinary state school, the Head has on several occasions taken retarded and maladjusted children into her school and has shown a marked degree of success with these children.

When Andrew was admitted to the school he was very depressed and withdrawn. He did not join in activities and during the first half-term did not speak at all. The first relationship he formed was with the Head—not by speaking, but by touching her spectacles. After a while, he removed the spectacles from the Head's face, putting them on himself for a moment, then returning them to the Head. Eventually he began to answer in monosyllables and then started to approach another child in his class—first of all simply by watching what the child was doing, then joining in by handing bricks or other equipment to him. While he was forming this relationship, he did not visit the Head's room at all. (He had previously been in the habit of walking out of the class into the Head's office.) It seemed as if he could not hold the first relationship while forming the second. After the holiday, he was again very morose and withdrawn, but resumed his relationship with the Head fairly quickly.

When Andrew was seven years old, he did not transfer to the junior school, because it was assessed that he was operating at about the level of a four-year-old. He stayed in the infant school until 1967, when he was admitted to a special E.S.N. school. At his time, his IQ was assessed at 55+, but this was stated to be probably an under-estimate, due to difficulty in administering the tests because he was still extremely withdrawn with strangers.

It was fortunate that my visits to the school coincided with a period when Andrew began to show marked improvement, and this became evident in his movement as well as in his speech. This will be discussed at more length in the appropriate sections.

Body aspects

When I first started to visit the school, the most noticeable thing about Andrew was his almost complete immobility for considerable periods. Generally, anyone sitting or standing 'still', whether a child or an adult, shifts his position, however slightly, from time to time, and also makes small shadow movements. Andrew, however, seemed to remain completely still, generally with an air of heaviness about him. He never spoke first and answered wherever possible by nodding or shaking his head. His body shape was withdrawn with a backward stress and his gestures were mainly of a gathering nature, inwards to the body.

At the beginning of my observations, I wrote in my notes that Andrew appeared to have the ability to concentrate on one thing for a considerable period of time. After watching him on several occasions, however, I felt that in some instances he was not really conscious of the activity and his thoughts were far removed from the task in hand. An example of this was one occasion when he was building with a construction set, and certainly, at first, he was concentrating; he looked directly at the work and his movements were direct and purposeful. After a while, I noticed that, although he kept moving one or two of the parts and appeared to be looking at the model, his eyes were not really focusing on the work at all. Also, although his hand and arm were moving, the rest of his body had become very passive and heavy. This pattern of behaviour was the same on several occasions and I wondered if in the past he had found that provided he appeared to be engrossed in some activity, he was left alone, and therefore used an outward show of activity as a form of barrier.

Towards the end of the first term that I visited the school, Andrew had become less withdrawn, not only with me, but generally with the rest of the children and the members of the staff. There were occasions when he would suddenly draw himself up straight and look about the room as if he were aware, not only of the other people in the room, but of himself in relationship to them. It was also about this time that he made an engine with a construction set and for the first time brought it to me, showing me how he had made it. He proceeded to play with it on the floor, pushing it along and moving in the room quite freely.

Effort

Andrew's movements are mainly strong and sustained, but reducing in strength and, when space effort is used, direct. Sustainment is one of the most important features and I rarely saw him make a sudden movement. He uses varying degrees of bound flow, but rarely uses a completely free-flowing movement.

On one occasion, I was able to watch Andrew from the staffroom window during an afternoon break and it was interesting to see that he appeared to be experimenting with different ways of walking. He first put a deliberate accent on one leg then on the other. He then tried stamping along, both feet being stamped down equally firmly. Sometimes, he took large strides and at other times very tiny steps. It was almost as if he was discovering different ways of walking and was aware only of his feet, where they were going and how they were moving.

Although Andrew uses mainly strength with a tendency to decrease into heaviness, he can and does use fine touch when using his hands, although he still often becomes heavier and moves away from the fineness of touch, with sustainment.

On one occasion, he was modelling a monster-type animal in Plasticine. He had moulded the original shape with strong, direct, sustained movements, but then began to use very fine movements for shaping and marking patterns, and it was while he was doing this that some suddenness came into his movements. An interesting feature of this monster was an enormous mouth into which Andrew fed a succession of small cars. I feel this probably had a psychological significance which would be understood and worked with by an expert therapist.

While Andrew was working on this model, and on many other occasions, he made continuous shadow movements of his face (strong/flexible/sustained). When reading to the teacher, Andrew made small circular movements with his right forefinger. This could perhaps be a sign of stress which in Andrew manifests itself in this type of movement or, perhaps, a type of 'superstitious' behaviour, which psychologists say arises when a person connects one activity with some form of success in another activity, even when there is no logical link. For example, if Andrew had been particularly praised for his reading one day while making these movements, he might associate them with his success.

Space

When I first started to visit the school, Andrew rarely moved away from his own table, and during movement sessions kept mainly in one place, always towards the back of the hall. He gradually began to move about the hall more easily and within the classroom he would now play with toys he had constructed on the floor, often pushing them slowly along and moving after them. Previously, he had played with such things only on his own table. He also started to stretch out to the limits of his own kinesphere more easily, although he still needed encouragement to stretch up on to his toes. His gradually increasing use of space seemed to coincide with his growing awareness of himself as a person and of himself in relationship both to other people and to the environment.

In his whole-body movements and when working with his hands, Andrew uses mainly direct movements. When painting and modelling and cutting out shapes he uses direct, angular designs rather than flexible curving shapes and he is meticulously careful in drawing and cutting out these shapes.

It appears that Andrew is rather averse to moving very freely in space. Although this has improved lately, he prefers moving near the ground and is certainly more direct in his movements. This directness is rather characteristic of him generally. He always moves as directly as possible from A to B and is very direct in his speech, saying exactly what he wants to and then stopping. His manner of speech is very clear and pronounced, maybe because of his prolonged visits to a speech therapist in his early childhood. As there is an almost complete lack of flexibility, I wonder if there is a danger of mental inflexibility, and if this will cause any additional problems in the future?

Relationships

Forming relationships is, of course, one of Andrew's major problems and, as explained in more detail in the section on his background, this was the first problem which had to be faced when he was originally admitted to the infant school.

He is still coming to terms with this problem and his progress seems to be made in short spurts. Although he is inclined to regress afterwards, he does not completely lose the ground gained, but only slips back a little.

When I first started to visit the school, it took several visits before Andrew would even return a smile. He would then answer questions about his work and, finally, after a fairly lengthy period, would bring up work to me, moving away from his desk to do so. When I had been absent for a period, I wondered if my relationship with him would have disappeared completely, but in fact it took only about three weeks to get back to the stage we had already reached. This could have been partly because now I knew Andrew, whereas when I first started to visit, not only did Andrew have to get to know me, but I had to get to know him. In addition, Andrew had made marked progress during this period. The Deputy Head related to me with great satisfaction a story of what had happened when Andrew had been taken swimming with a small group of boys. Apparently, the Deputy Head was in the water with the boys and had told Andrew he would be with him in a moment to help him. After a short while, Andrew obviously felt he had been kept waiting long enough and actually shouted at the Deputy Head: 'Come on—I'm still waiting!' I wonder if it was the sensation of buoyancy in the water which had a releasing effect on Andrew? Whatever the reason, it was regarded as an important stage in his progress that Andrew could be verbally aggressive, even to this extent. Note the connection between the lack of relationships, and (a) bodily immobility, (b) inward-flowing and narrow movement, and (c) lack of active flow content in his movement.

JIMMY: AGED EIGHT

Jimmy is a bright eight-year-old at a junior school. Somehow I knew from the very first meeting that Jimmy would be my choice. 'A poor little fellow!' I thought. He was untidy in appearance, wearing a grey shirt, when most boys wore white ones, tie askew, and with an outsize sheriff's badge pinned to the lapel of a well-worn blazer. He was a thin little boy with very pale skin and untidy blonde hair to his shoulders, but the face under this hair was alive; his eager, alert blue eyes were interested in everything around him; his thin lips easily broadened into a very attractive smile. This 'poor little fellow', I since find, has two elder sisters, a mother who is a co-director of a large firm, and a father who is a lecturer in psychology.

Jimmy moves from the centre of levity and is concerned only with the top half of his body. He is very loose-limbed and yet in a movement lesson he does not appear to be aware of his extremities at all. He has a 'dream-like' quality and during the first lesson appeared to show caution, always slow to start, and following others rather than depending on himself. His body awareness was not good. At the command 'Hands on the floor in front of you!' Jimmy's hands went behind. Jimmy obviously enjoyed jumping, but when asked 'Jump with your knees to your nose' he did not bother with the task set. He didn't bend his body at all, but jumped with knees under him.

He enjoys moving in the space around the room. He appears to hesitate, starting with bound flow, and then, when he has gained confidence, zooming into free flow, finding difficulty in stopping. His feet and legs take him, but he is not aware of them: space and the top half of the body are important to him. His body and arms are held symmetrically when he runs. His arms are not involved in the movement. At certain times, his arms appear to be uncoordinated. During the first visit to College, they seemed to hang very awkwardly; it was at this time that his eyes were 'all over the place' and he found it difficult to become absorbed. On the second visit, it was only occasionally noticeable that his arms hung strangely and did not seem to belong to his body. In the school playground he does not appear to have this problem of coordination. Could it be that this awkwardness is part of a personal uninvolvement and feeling of insecurity?

A 'wall' body shape is very natural to Jimmy. He likes the top half of his body to be open and shows this clearly in the way he demonstrates the pin, ball and twisted body shapes. He turns round, left side leading into an open turn, and when asked to reverse the turn, he repeats himself to the left again. He is right-handed and leads with his right foot. He has not acquired good ball skill with his hands, but is a promising footballer with a strong, direct, right-footed kick. He is capable at gymnastics, which he enjoys and, surprisingly enough, shows no fear or caution. His body has an 'india-rubber' quality, which lacks coordination. He finds balancing difficult, yet he makes a good attempt at walking on his hands.

Jimmy appears to enjoy movement better among a small number when distraction is not so great. During dramatic movement with two other children, Jimmy was excellent—completely absorbed, even to the extent of using his own voice sounds.

Jimmy is an energetic, nimble, light mover. However, he does not seem able to find strength and, when asked to hold a strong shape, his light movement peters out. Even so, his lightness appears to be on an 'even keel', for although strength eludes him he cannot adjust his degree of lightness to attain a very fine touch.

He is very aware of time and enjoys quick, lively, darting movements. Then he becomes so free that he cannot exert control. When he is unsure, either of himself or of the task set, he considers carefully, indulging in time, then moves with bound flow, changing into free flow when his confidence is regained. Whatever he eventually attempts is direct and to the point, but the phrasing is puzzling. The initial hesitation before directness might show a preference for impactive phrasing, but there is no 'holding' at the end. On the other hand, if Jimmy did not give such prolonged thought to the task, he could, without doubt, be an impulsive mover—a good beginning petering into a very weak end.

This impulsiveness was confined during clay modelling, where Jimmy had marvellous ideas; he would make a giraffe or a tiger in a cage or a dog, but somehow they never materialised. Eventually, he produced a knife, a fork and a mug. (The narrow shapes he produced were interesting, for even the mug was modelled on a stem.) Two weeks later, during a school visit, Jimmy was given clay to produce a pot. It was a good effort, showing a good definite base, but petering away at the edges, having an almost unfinished appearance about it.

Jimmy is a very sensitive little boy. His sensitivity showed during a 'making music' session. He was at once drawn to the chime bars. He hit them delicately and was fascinated and delighted by the tone produced. When given two chime bars and the task of playing each one according to the chord fingering on a guitar, he was very attentive, followed well, and kept good time. He has quite a good rhythmic sense and understands the various qualities in music, as is seen from his chalk rhythms.

Sensitivity is also shown when he paints. He never uses strong colours and takes great care to water the paint well, giving his work a delicate pastel quality. He does not bend over his work, but sits symmetrically wide, at right-angles to the paper, taking a light hold on the brush and appearing to ponder deeply. Then he proceeds to shape the action of painting to the air before actually dipping his brush carefully into the pastel shade and putting paint on paper. He tends to 'dream', as if in a world of his own. Then, towards the end of his work, he loses interest and needs encouragement to finish it.

His painting shows a good use of space. Jimmy likes to have plenty of room and cannot bear to be hemmed in. During the movement sessions, one of the reasons why he was always last in settling in a space was because he was so fussy and selective. He always kept to the outer area of the gymnasium and never went into the centre.

He enjoys moving high but seems equally at home low. He runs wide and open, with his hands always out to the side. When given the task of tracing the first initial of his name in the air, he used his arms and shoulders extensively in his own sphere of movement, and didn't venture beyond it. For some reason he found this difficult. He made four attempts at the task and appeared very disjointed and jerky.

He thoroughly enjoys the flight of his body through the air when running and leaping in space, but somehow, although he gains height with the top half of his body, he is not aware of the bottom half. He is happier at the feeling of covering ground. He is not 'at home' in restricted space nor does he like producing a 'pin' body shape. When given the task of crawling through a very narrow tunnel, he started with a low wide body shape, rather than narrow, wormed his way forward with the top half of his body and then immediately rose to his knees and stood up. He said: 'I don't have to be narrow, I'm thin enough!'

Jimmy, then, is adaptable and amenable, and works better with a smaller group than the whole class. Working just with two other children and myself, he was more easily absorbed and appeared ready and eager for whatever was programmed. He is not domineering and likes to be organised, being content to follow. He plays mainly with girls; he is led by Fiona, the girl he sits next to in class, whom he continually watches and copies. He doesn't ask for a lot of attention. He has a wide vocabulary for his age and in conversation he is forthcoming and interesting, after initial shyness. He is gifted with a vivid imagination, is good at inventing stories and excellent at drama. Why is it, then, that at times he found such difficulty in being absorbed in the movement lessons? Was it merely his interest in everything and everybody around him which made concentration difficult, or does he have a feeling of insecurity?

Conclusions

Although I have come to the end of this child study with many unanswered questions, I now feel even more strongly that the art of movement can play an important, perhaps vital, part in helping children to develop as fully as possible. If children can gradually become involved in expressive movement which is meaningful to them, it will not only enable them to experience movement qualities undiscoverable in their everyday life, but with increased body awareness—which springs from, and contributes to, the sense of 'self'—they will perhaps be able to build up the self-confidence they so badly need.

I have also been made aware of how much can be learned from observing children moving, and how an essential part of this knowledge comes from a growing personal understanding and questioning of my inner attitudes and reactions. This first became apparent in trying to understand why I found some children more interesting and indeed easier to observe than others. The reason for this must surely rest not only in the children but also in my own attitude and reaction to them. We sometimes say that we 'took to' a person straight-away', or the opposite, and in many instance this snap judgement is made even before we speak to the person concerned. We must, therefore, be judging them on their movement, body attitudes, and so on, and by the way our own inner attitudes are affected by them.

I am left, then, with questions, not only about the children I have studied, but also the implications of such questions as applied to children generally; and probably most important of all, their implications concerning myself and my inner attitudes, as reflected in the way I observe other people.

Review of literature

Many researchers have been aware that the way a person moves is indicative of his individuality—no two people walk, make gestures, or move their bodies in exactly the same way. Certainly, similarities have been observed between members of the same family (for instance, Prince Charles's body carriage and the way in which he holds his hands behind his back as he walks, have been commented upon as being like the body carriage of the Duke of Edinburgh); between racial groups (see Efron's research described later); and between cultural groups (see Argyle's work, also described later); but within these broad categories, the individual traits are still apparent and discernible. For instance, we recognise the sound of a friend's footsteps, because of the particular movement characteristics of the person; we recognise a 'backview' of a walk or stance long before we are able to see the features of distinctive facial qualities we know.

Researchers have used this knowledge for diagnostic and clinical purposes, either as a means by which an analyst understands his patient better (see later reference to Laing and Szekely) or as a help in understanding and analysing the Rorschach-test (Schachtel's work on this is mentioned later.) The relationships of babies with their mothers have been understood, not only through the backward-looking memory of adults, but also through directly observing the infant. This is an area for future research which the more detailed understanding of movement and its recording, described here, will be able to help, and which is already under way in a pilot-scheme stage.[1]

Therapeutic techniques have been developed which are based on the belief that changing the bodily movement will

[1] M. North, private research.

effect a change of the personality (see later reference to Barlow, Alexander and Reich).

The typing of so-called 'normal' persons by movement characteristics is well known (see later reference to Sheldon and Parnell) and attempts have been made to categorise mental illness as well as bodily disabilities by movement characteristics (see later references to Krout on autistic children).

In grouping the above-named specialists from different disciplines who have attempted to use movement to further their research, it is necessary to refer to physiologists and neurologists (see, for example, Greenacre[2] and Preyer[3]); psychologists, either researchers or clinical (see later references to Murray, Lewin, Allport, Fisher and Cleveland [on body image]; Sheldon, Parnell, Szekely, Laing and Ruesch); sociologists and anthropologists (Efron, Hall, Argyle, Goffman and Mead); and artists and scientists (Leach and Einstein). Moreover, these do not cover all the people who, consciously or unconsciously, study movement and apply it for their greater understanding of people.

No published statement claims that there is any direct connection between movement characteristics and intelligence. To the writer's knowledge, her research is the first investigation into such a hypothesis. It is made possible as the result of practical experience over many years and the recognition that certain movement characteristics seem to appear in the more intelligent people who have been observed in detail. It is generally recognised that personality traits and characteristics can be traced through the movement of the individual, and current research is attempting to locate those aspects of movement which, while being indicative of personality, are significantly related to intelligence.

The following detailed descriptions of research involving movement study indicate the need for a more exact observational technique, and system of recording movement, qualitatively and quantitatively, which can be supplied by Laban's method of analysis. The time has come for movement

[2] P. Greenacre, *Trauma, Growth and Personality*, Hogarth Press 1953.
[3] W. Preyer, *Embrionic Motility and Sensitivity*, Monographs of the Society for Research in Child Development (Washington) 1937.

specialists and other workers in the various fields outlined to pool their knowledge and skills, so that movement practitioners may cease to be so isolated from the other disciplines, and specialists of all these types may have access to a system which will help to further their research and practice.

Michael Balint comments: 'When looking up the literature about it, I was surprised to find how little is known about the psychology of movement'.[4] It is, then, as if the whole area of movement has been tentatively looked over, but never systematically explored. Charlotte Woolf,[5] for example, did pioneer work in drawing attention to the significance of gestures, but she limited her observations to the pattern and shape of gesture in isolated movements, so missing the significance of rhythm, phrase and quality, as well as the relatedness of gesture to other body movement. However, she states quite clearly: 'It is the fleeting and scarcely tangible expressions of gestures which unmask a man. Here we have a language conveying by continual and secret messages the essence of personality.' These 'scarcely tangible expressions' can now be observed, analysed, and recorded accurately.

Cyril Burt has said; 'In the activities both of the school and of ordinary life, kinaesthetic discrimination (in popular discussion often described as a form of touch) plays a far greater part than is commonly realised; but strange to say, hardly any factorial studies have been attempted on this process.'[6] Again, then, the need for research into the relationships between movement and personality is pointed out. Support for the existence of this relationship, not from research but from experience, comes from artists and scientists alike. Bernard Leach has said in a lecture: 'I make a pot with my whole body.' Einstein observed that his scientific thinking did not occur in verbal images, but in the form of optical and kinaesthetic images of movement: 'Verbalisation is only the final and very laborious work of editing.'[7]

[4] Michael Balint, *Thrills and Regressions*, Hogarth Press 1959.
[5] Charlotte Woolf, *The Psychology of Gesture*, Methuen 1945.
[6] C. Burt, 'The Structure of the Mind' in *Intelligence and Ability* ed. Stephen Wiseman, Penguin Modern Psychology, and *British Journal of Educational Psychology*, 19, 1949.
[7] J. Hadamard, 'An Essay in the Psychology of Invention in the Mathematical Field', Princeton University Press 1945.

Others make similar comments, but seem to have recognised them from observing other people, whereas Einstein's observations came from his own bodily experience. Surely, though, it is only through relating such observation of others to personal bodily experience that they can be understood and verbalised. Many of the observations and interpretations made by therapists, doctors and analysts are intuitive, and based on personal experiences. These interpretations need not be any the less accurate because of this, though it does depend, as does all everyday recognition of movement in others, on the particular sensitivity (or sensibility) of the observer. Sensibility enables him to relate the movement he sees to the kinaesthetic experiences which he himself has known. If he has also understood these experiences, he may be able to interpret their meaning with reference to himself and others.

The relationship between kinaesthetic awareness (of movement in the sense used in this book) and thought processes and inner feelings is clearly recognised by the Swedish psychoanalyst, Dr Szekely, when he discusses the 'creative pause' which is often necessary in life before finding solutions to problems, or making an imaginative leap in art or science.[8] He puts forward the ideas that 'the operation of thought develops from internalised action', and 'in many persons thought-contents are not verbalised, but are realised consciously in actions as the kinaesthetic perception of movement, or as the optical perception of the movement of foreign bodies.'

The Rorschach-test, though dependent on patients' co-operation in answering questions, or at least reacting to inkblots, also uses the psychologists' observation of a patient's movement during the test.

E. Schachtel[9] enjoins the psychologist not only to take account of reported movement in the patient's responses to the inkblots, but to observe directly the actual bodily movements and responses of the patient. He points out that a

[8] L. Szekely, 'The Creative Pause', *International Journal of Psychoanalysis*, vol. 48, part 3, pp. 353-67.
[9] E. Schachtel, *Experimental Foundations of Rorschach's Test*, Tavistock 1967.

patient's verbal description of his bodily sensations, movement feelings or experiences may well be distorted, and may omit or misinterpret what actually happened. Only direct, immediate observation of the patient by a skilled observer can accurately balance these statements.

Similarly, R.D. Laing, in his example of a 'double bind' in communication, points out how different messages can be conveyed by words and by the movement accompanying the words. For instance, there is the case of a mother greeting her son who is recovering from a mental breakdown: 'As he goes towards her

1   she opens her arms for him to embrace her, and/or

2   to embrace him

3   as he gets nearer, she freezes and stiffens

4   he stops irresolutely

5   she says "Don't you want to kiss your Mummy?" and as he still stands irresolutely

6   she says "But, dear, you mustn't be afraid of your feelings."

Thus he is responding to her invitation to kiss her, but her posture, freezing, tension, simultaneously tell him not to do.'[10]

These kinds of signals in movement, supporting or conflicting with the words we use, occur all the time—producing a feeling of reassurance (if supporting) or confusion (if conflicting) in the child or other person. Ruesch and Kees have said: 'Any message may be regarded as having two aspects, the statement proper and the explanations pertaining to its interpretation.'[11] The verbal and non-verbal combine, then, to make meaning clearer or more complicated.

In communication with anyone, it is necessary to take into account this 'double language'. Infants and young children are entirely dependent upon movement language, and there are many current research projects on infant behaviour in this country, in the USA and in Canada. Many observers are content to use mechanical observation procedures—for example, they count how many times within a given period an infant cries, looks at his mother during

[10] R.D. Laing, *The Self and Others* p. 139 Tavistock 1961.
[11] J. Ruesch and W. Kees, *Non-Verbal Communication*, University of California Press 1956.

feeding, and so on, or what body shapes and actions are made in accompanying the crying, laughing and feeding.

A few people have attempted more qualitative observations and Dr J.S. Kestenberg,[12] neurologist and psychoanalyst, has published three papers relating to early behaviour in infants. These papers develop ideas which relate specific movement patterns to stages of child development. I. Bartenieff, a therapist in New York,[13] has also recorded her preliminary studies into infant movement behaviour. Both of these investigations use a modified version of movement analysis and notation which has been developed in this country. Dr Kestenberg tends to adapt her observations to a preconceived formulation of psychoanalytical theory of infant and child development. Bartenieff parallels physiological growth patterns with movements. The comments are general and somewhat over-simplified. In a later article,[14] Kestenberg discusses two rhythmical patterns of body movement: (a) rising and falling tensions; and (b) movement towards and away from the body. These are then related to two phases of development: 6-12 months, and the second year of life.

As early as 1872, Charles Darwin[15] described movement and expression in man and animals, and since then many psychologists, attempting to assess personality, have frequently mentioned the significance of movement (among them, P.E. Vernon,[16] G.W. Allport,[17] P. Schilder,[18]

[12] J.S. Kestenberg, *Psycho Analytic Quarterly* (New York) 34, 35 and 36; has studied in this country with Warren Lamb and with the author.

[13] I. Bartenieff, *Unity of Expression and Function*, Monograph 1965. Like Kestenberg, this author has also studied here with Laban, Lamb and the present author.

[14] J.S. Kestenberg, 'Rhythm and Organisation in Obsessive Compulsive Development', *International Journal of Psychoanalysis*, 47, 1966.

[15] C. Darwin, *The Expression of the Emotions in Man and Animal*, Murray 1872.

[16] P.E. Vernon, *Personality Assessment*, Methuen 1964.

[17] G.W. Allport, *Personality: A Psychological Interpretation*, Constable 1938; *Personality and Social Encounter*, Beacon Press, Boston 1960; *Pattern and Growth in Personality*, Holt Rinehart, New York 1961; G.W. Allport and P.E. Vernon, *Studies in Expressive Movement*, Hafner 1967.

[18] P. Schilder, *The Image and Appearance of the Human Body*, Kegan Paul 1935.

M. Feldenkraus,[19] F.J.J. Buytendijk,[20] H.A. Murray,[21] Kurt Lewin[22] and W.H. Sheldon.[23] Mostly, they mention movement as an adjunct to their main studies, frequently making the comment that no real tool of observation and analysis of movement is available. For instance, H.A. Murray states that, since psychology deals with processes occurring in time, 'none of its proper study can be static, all must be dynamic.' He gives a formula, speaking in terms of process, of a 'beginning situation', 'action pattern' ('actone') and 'end situation'. He decides, however, to study the beginning end situations only, and so, by selecting the static and avoiding the 'action pattern', he goes against his own statement, leaving out the essential factor, the process. This leads him to concentrate on needs, ends and stimuli, both inner and outer. He sees the 'actone', when related to ends, as functional, and when related to beginnings, as expressive. This was in 1938, and although much talk has gone on since then, there is still little work on the process, except as a result of Laban's work.

Kurt Lewin, also working on the idea of action process, discovered that it is not an uninterrupted flow, but continues in stages, growing one stage upon another. He stressed pathways, and the need to vary spatial patterns in relation to external and environmental obstacles—'detour of behaviour', as he termed this.

C. Allport comes nearer to relating movement to individual personality, but still lacks the means, namely, a 'language' of movement, to develop the links which he clearly sees. Among his many theories and explorations of motivations, spontaneity, and so on, he describes his theory of traits, or basic elements of personality common to all people.

[19] M. Feldenkrais, *Body and Mature Behaviour*, Routledge 1949.
[20] F.J.J. Buytendijk, *Mensch und Tier*, Hamburg 1958.
[21] H.A. Murray, *Explorations in Personality*, Harvard University Press 1938.
[22] K. Lewin, *A Dynamic Theory of Personality*, McGraw-Hill (New York) 1935.
[23] W.H. Sheldon and S. Stevens, *The Varieties of Temperament and Psychological Study*, Harper (New York) 1942; *Varieties of Human Physique*, Harper (New York) 1940; W.H. Sheldon, *The Atlas of Man*, Harper (New York) 1954.

The list is extensive, and covers terms characterising personal behaviour and personality, for instance:

1 Neutral terms, designating personal traits (examples: abrupt, absent-minded, etc.)
2 Terms primarily descriptive of temporary moods or activities (examples: abashed, absorbed, accusing, etc.)
3 Weighted terms conveying social or character judgements on personal conduct, or designating influence on others (examples: absurd, acceptable, acclaimed, etc.)
4 Miscellaneous: descriptions of physique, capacities and developmental conditions, metaphorical and doubtful terms (examples: abrasive, abstract, abysmal, etc.)

He is aware of the problem of classifying movement and attempts to separate 'those aspects of movement which are objectively measurable from those that can be described only in qualitative terms'.

Allport tries to get at the meaning of movement in a very precise way, but he lacks a means of describing movement itself, falling back upon descriptive words, which are poetic and colourful but unfortunately consist of a complex of many different patterns, phrases and processes of movement. He sees the movement and leaps to the interpretation of it, missing out the detailed description and recording of the movement itself, which would illuminate and, to a great extent, clarify the verbal descriptions.

Now that there is a tool for accurate descriptions of movement and the notation to record it, much of this rather generalised descriptive work is unnecessary, though it seems that, for interpreting the movement notation, Allport's choice and selection of words could help to make the meaning of movement more meaningful to others.

The work of Sheldon and Parnell[24] has been developed by Dr Tanner and Dr Barlow in this country, and relates mainly to the grouping of personality types and behaviour in accordance with physical types, i.e.

[24] R.W. Parnell, *Behaviour and Physique*, Edward Arnold 1958.

Endomorph ('Viscerontonia') e.g. relaxed, sloppy and slow;
Mesomorph ('Somatotonia') e.g. assertive, dominant, explosive;
Ectomorph ('Cerebrotonia') e.g. meticulous, lonely, 'thinker'.

The detailed descriptions of these three basic types include many references to movement, patterns, styles and actions, though again, only in verbal descriptions.

The treatment of patients' psychological disorders through the improvement of physical stance, posture, easing of tensions, and so forth, seems to connect with the work relating to attitude psychology. Nina Bull[25] claims that research into reactions of subjects under hypnosis proves that emotion is a direct result of body attitude. While her published research does not seem to justify such a positive claim (nor do the subsequent theories based on her assumption), the experiments under hypnosis nevertheless support the general agreement that the body and mind are inextricably united and that movements in one are reflected in the other. Such medical research enlarges our understanding of human movement and its significance.[26]

The influence of the body over the mind was known to exist by the ancients; primitive tribes and religious groups have traditionally used such changes of body positions, as well as movement patterns and rhythms, to induce a change of mood or inner attitude. For instance, the Dervish group of Sufi adherents is well known for its whirling and turning dances, inducing an altered state of consciousness as surely as drug treatment, and many tribes have induced hypnosis, or a heightened state of awareness, through their knowledge of

[25] Nina Bull, *The Body and Its Mind (An Introduction to Attitude Psychology)*, Americas Publishing Co. 1962.
[26] Eminent doctors and professors are quoted by Nina Bull as supporting this theory. My own reaction is that these neurologists tend to see the body as the initiator of inner emotion, but, unless they have other data, not published in this book, I cannot see that, by proving that a person cannot feel and express an emotion without at the same time changing his body attitude, one says any more than that the body and its emotions are two facets of the same experience. How do they account for a person being aroused emotionally and such arousal resulting in a particular body attitude?

movement. The Yorobi tribe has many different religious cults, from which each person can select the style and ritual and type most suited to his personality (such as the trickster-god, the all-powerful, dominant father figure, etc.) However, ritual and dance is not limited to primitive peoples, for teenagers in our own culture use rhythm or beat and music or sound very much in the same way as do the primitive tribes, in order to be 'taken out of' themselves.

In a somewhat different category are the therapy techniques which deliberately manipulate the body for purposes of manipulating the mind.

The 'bio-energetic' therapy practised by followers of Reich[27] is based on direct manipulation of the body, changing the body stance, tensions, and so on; and thereby its practitioners 'release inner tensions'. There is a complicated theory of what ideally the body-mind relationship should be. Generally, it seems to be assumed that tension is 'bad'. The techniques of Feldenkrais[28] and Alexander[29] are also based on direct bodily action, breathing, position, and so on. The criticism of these techniques is directed towards the assumption that tensions are necessarily bad, and that the way in which the body/mind has defended itself against those experiences which have created the observable distortions is a 'bad thing'. To break down these defences without being aware of their values, perhaps as some kind of war of psychic survival, leaves the individual open and vulnerable, at best, a transference of symptoms can occur, either to another body part, or to the mind. Nevertheless, a good practitioner will offer understanding and the opportunity for self-help to the patient, and this may genuinely influence the disturbance.

Psychoanalytic theory recognises clear links between the body action of patients and their mental or emotional states. Felix Deutsch quoted Freud's idea of the 'mysterious leap' from the psychic to the physiologic, and said, in 1959: 'But to this very day, we are still far from closing the "mysterious leap".[30] While the references here are to bodily illness, as

[27] W. Reich, *Character Analysis*, Vision Publications 1950.
[28] M. Feldenkrais, *op. cit.*
[29] F.M. Alexander, *Man's Supreme Inheritance; Constructive Conscious Behaviour of the Individual*, Methuen 1910.
[30] Felix Deutsch, ed. *On the Mysterious Leap from the Mind to the*

distinct from posture or patterns of gesture, there are many movement implications in states such as hysteria, which involve the whole body/mind.

A clear example of the effect of a mental or emotional illness on the bodily actions and gestures can be seen in any mental hospital (in the static, rigid patient, and the violent, aggressive one). In these days, of course, many of the obvious patterns of movement are diminished by drugs. The lethargic 'glazed' movement of a drug-addict or patient is an easily recognised as that of the uncontrolled alcoholic. Autistic children are often first recognised because of their typical and repetitive patterns of behaviour and body action.[31]

Bettelheim says, in discussing the literature on autistic children by Hergman and Escalons (1949), that 'While the authors speak here mainly of a barrier to sensory stimuli, I shall assume this refers equally to emotional stimuli, since at this early age (i.e. infants) it makes little sense to differentiate between the two.'[32] Most sensitive observers of children, and most doctors and analysts of the calibre of Bettelheim, realise how inadequate it is to deal with physical symptoms or movement without relation to the emotional experiences inherent in and resulting from the physical.

Sociologists and anthropologists are particularly concerned with cultural patterns, communication and expression. Professor Ray Birdwhistell describes communication and sign-language: 'As anthropologists have become increasingly aware of the importance of comparative body motion studies, evidence has accumulated to support the proposition that "gestures" are culture-linked both in shape and meaning.'[33] David Efron,[34] in 1941, gave evidence that this was so through his studies with two immigrant groups in New

Body: A Workshop Study on the Theory of Conversion, International Universities Press (New York) 1959.

[31] M.H. Krout, 'Autistic Gestures', *Psychological Monographs, Psychological Review* (New York) 1935. *R.W. Zazlow, Journal of Educational Psychology,* No. 57, 1966.

[32] B. Bettelheim, *The Empty Fortress,* Free Press (New York) 1959.

[33] R.L. Birdwhistell, 'Communication without Words'. Draft of manuscript for *L'Aventure Humaine,* Eastern Pennsylvania Psychiatric Institute 1964; *Kinesics and Communication,* Carpenter & McLin 1960.

[34] D. Efron, *Gesture and Environment,* King's Crown Press (New York) 1941.

York. He studied the gestures of Eastern European Jews and Southern Italians living in New York City, from the point of view of body activity and spatial patterns, on a time continuum. In this way he described characteristic racial movements. When these groups spoke American, their gesture patterns changed to those typical of American culture, that is, they had two languages and two sets of gestures, each relating to the language being spoken.

This recognition of broad cultural differences in movement does not detract from the contention that the subtle personal differences can also be discerned within the general style, just as a person cannot disguise his handwriting from an expert graphologist, even when using a stylised script. It would be interesting to make personal-movement records of Efron's subjects while speaking each language, to show how the basic patterns of rhythmical alternations, stresses and qualities remain, reflecting the uniqueness of each person.

Birdwhistell himself goes on to describe ways in which personal variations can be discerned, but again only in verbal, descriptive language. A salute may be performed 'in a manner which could satisfy, please or enrage the most demanding officer. By shifts in stance, in facial expression, in the velocity or duration of the movement of salutation, and even in the selection of inappropriate contexts for the act, the soldier could dignify, ridicule, demean, seduce, insult or promote his *vis-à-vis.*' But on further investigation, it appears that it is not these subtle personal differences which Professor Birdwhistell investigates further, but how to classify and codify movement in a way similar to the codification of language. This follows closely the behaviourist school of psychology, and his research shows clear parallels between verbal language (as understood by the behaviourist) and the language of movement. The patterns of movement, he calls 'kinesics': 'The systematic study of how human beings communicate through body movement and gesture.' This is certainly one way of developing further a detailed knowledge of movement from the measurable aspects. It is concerned with possible physical actions, their range, extension, duration, and intensity. Much of the analysis has been based on work from slow-motion films, giving opportunity for detailed spatial and bodily observation and accuracy. Already, cultural differences in these aspects of movement have been clearly shown; Americans have a range of movement patterns different from, say, those of the English.

Edward Hall,[35] Michael Argyle,[36] and J. Ruesch[37] are interested in non-verbal communications, and have detailed some aspects of the 'silent language'.

Hall describes the significance of distance between two interacting people. Each culture has clearly defined distances which operate when two people talk; when people from two different cultures meet, the differences in their ideas of exactly how far apart they should be can cause embarrassment, unease and friction, even if the verbal language problems can be overcome. Argyle says, for example: 'Americans and Europeans have been seen retreating backwards or gyrating in circles at international conferences, pursued by Latin Americans trying to establish their habitual degree of proximity.'

Argyle includes body positions, gestures, facial expressions and eye movements as vital elements of what he calls 'social techniques'. He takes the view that these are learned and repeated because they have been successful in the past, that is, successful in eliciting the desired reponses from others. Communication through 'eye contact', probably the most observed and tabulated infant-mother relationship,[38] is described by Argyle in detail. The holding of eye contact and its duration, and the avoiding of gaze, both play a special part in a conversation. He suggests that we tend to look directly when confident over what we are saying, and to avert our gaze when hesitating and collecting thoughts, and to regain eye contact to show we have finished speaking.

Argyle further develops the idea of the 'kinesic dance', that is, the interaction between people through one observing how the other moves, as well as listening to what he is saying

[35] Edward Hall, *The Silent Language*, Doubleday (New York) 1959.
[36] Michael Argyle, *The Psychology of Interpersonal Behaviour*, Penguin Books 1967, 1971.
[37] J. Ruesch, *op. cit.*
[38] A film, *Early Mother–Baby Relationships*, has been made by Dr Donald Gough on eye contact between infants and mothers during feeding, and is distributed by Concord Films Council, Nacton, Ipswich.

(see also Goffman[39]). For instance, lack of confidence quickly appears if, during a conversation between two people, one cannot see all of the other person's movements (as when he is wearing dark glasses and his eye movements cannot be seen). Apparently, from experiments, it is more useful for the face to be seen than the eyes alone. This is not surprising, as the whole facial expression gives complex 'clues', just as the body itself, in its adjustments, positions and tensions, adds to the whole impact of a statement. Argyle states also from experiments that 'for males, vision is used in the coordination of bodily movements in a kinesic dance—females clearly make more use of visual information for feedback purposes.' This statement was based on the finding that 'females preferred to see the other even when invisible themselves . . . males did not—when invisible, they preferred not to see the other.'

Goffman, a sociologist, is also interested in the interaction between people, and uses dramatic terms for some of his movement ideas. He has studied the way that a person presents himself to others, like an actor to an audience, and how he tries to influence others in their information about him. His picture is of an individual 'managing' his self-presentation, using appropriate techniques in an on-going process, that is, in an 'information game', where information is 'given' and 'given off' by the 'actor'. Expressions which the actor 'gives' are intentional and usually verbal; expressions 'given off' are usually unintentional and non-verbal.[40] He elaborates on the forward and backward action between actor and audience (one individual and another) and estimates that the observation and understanding of the audience is more acute than the actor's ability to manipulate his behaviour.

The idea of influencing others through our own movement is well known. We all experience how we can 'pick up' the mood or attitude of another, and this is particularly strong in a group—for instance, hysteria, excitement and depression. (This is, of course, linked with the effect of movement deliberately used in primitive ritual, worship or politics which has been mentioned previously.

[39] Erving Goffman, *The Presentation of Self in Everyday Life*, Doubleday Anchor (New York) 1959.
[40] See also R.D. Laing, *op. cit.*

Movement and Meaning,[41] one of the latest books on movement, describes the significance of movement from historical and sociological viewpoints, but detailed description is hindered by a lack of movement notation and analysis.

Margaret Mead,[42] G. Kurath,[43] and Alan Lomax,[44] together with other anthropologists, all relate movement patterns, particularly as seen in rituals and dances, to the culture they are studying. Dr Mead has described dance forms, but not the everyday movement patterns. Kurath has studied, not only the dances, but everyday movement, working-action patterns, the handling of infants, and so on, notating them in movement notation (Labanotation). Lomax leads a team of investigators in a study of primitive cultures through their music and dance, a 'cantometrics project', using both effort notation and Labanotation to record the movement.

This brief survey of the literature and research relevant to movement study shows that there is a considerable interest and awareness of the significance of movement in human life, and the necessity for a deeper study of it. It seems that Laban's[45] contribution to these studies will become clearer as his initiative in developing a systematic study of the 'language of movement' which can be understood, experienced, observed, analysed, notated and described is applied to research. The main aspects of his work which are significant to the present book are 'summarised' in his notation systems. First, he recognised and categorised qualitative elements of movements which can be observed in all movement happenings. Secondly, he differentiated between qualitative and quantitative aspects—though these are always interconnected in human movement—which can be described directly in movement terms. Thirdly, he evolved a simple and

[41] E. Metheny, *Movement and Meaning*, McGraw-Hill (New York) 1968.
[42] Margaret Mead, *Coming of Age in Samoa*, republished by Penguin Books 1943.
[43] G. Kurath, 'Panorama of Dance Ethnology', *Current Anthropology* 1, May 1960.
[44] Alan Lomax, Professor of Columbia University, Anthropology Department.
[45] R. Laban, unpublished papers at the LAMC. Also *Effort*, Macdonald & Evans 1947, and *Mastery of Movement*, Macdonald & Evans 1950.

efficient notation system which enables an observer to record immediately not only quantitative but also qualitative movement. Recording had never been possible before, except by slow descriptive verbal language. Once the notation is recorded, it is available for future analysis, and includes pattern, rhythm, quality, shape and body participation.

Warren Lamb,[46] one of the earliest of Laban's pupils in Britain, has developed his own special way of adapting Laban's work to selection and training in industry. His book does not do justice to the quality of his work, nor does it fully describe his methods. Another book from him is long overdue.

It should now be clear that movement has been studied frequently by researchers from many different fields. One area of study not mentioned specifically so far is that of the significance of 'body image'. This term has been used in many different ways. Fisher and Cleveland[47] summarise the many attitudes of psychologists to this aspect of personality. 'Body awareness' (which includes body shapes and parts of the body used in each movement) is specifically related to certain aspects of 'body image'. The defining of such a relationship could be developed through further research.

[46] Warren Lamb, *Posture and Gesture*, Duckworth 1965.
[47] S. Fisher and S. Cleveland, *Body Image and Personality*, Dover Publications (New York) 1968.

Acknowledgements

It is easy to give acknowledgement to those people who have given specific help in the preparation of this book, and this I do gladly: to Dr J. Chandler, from San José, California, who during a private visit to this country spent time and energy in reading and correcting the script, and asking those questions which so pertinently drew attention to an inadequate explanation, or an implied assumption; to Teena Newman and Tony Key, both colleagues at Goldsmiths' College, who provided the illustrations; to the ILEA for photographs taken at Lucas Vale Primary School; to the children and staffs of the schools where the movement work was undertaken, and to Betty Stedman and Liz Braddock who kindly allowed their child studies to be included.

It is less easy to give credit to the many friends, colleagues and teachers who have contributed to my own ongoing education, so that this book could be written this year, but not last year, or the year before.

Prominent amongst the early influences on my work and personal development were Rudolf Laban, Lisa Ullman and Sylvia Bodmer, with whom I worked for many years. It was in Laban's outlook, his ways of considering movement, and his original work in the application of his knowledge of movement that the beginnings of my own movement understanding was rooted. After his death, I worked for many years in industry, therapy and education: in all of these areas of work I met with people who influenced my ability to use the knowledge I had in a more positive way, and this was a period of personal growth rather than an extension of movement knowledge. But in later years, I was fortunate in my university contacts, having a great deal to help in developing a system of research in children's movement which, although personally painful and demanding, helped me to clarify my thoughts and ideas. For this I would like to thank Professor Bantock at Leicester University. The development of the Advanced Diploma Course for experienced teachers, designed to develop the experience of practical movement and dance with the ability to relate psychological, sociological and philosophical understanding of the work, provided the students and myself with the opportunity to extend and deepen our personal involvement and experience. Here I must give my thanks especially to Dr M.D. Marshak, London University Institute of Education, who directed and nursed us through the course at the Institute, providing always a stimulating academic challenge, balanced by a penetrating insight into personal behaviour and relationships both in group seminars and in the dance itself. I have been particularly fortunate in having the chance to have many personal discussions with her. A new world of insight into the process of creativity generally, and its relevance to dance and dramatic movement was opened to the students and staff alike and I recognise the influence of these ideas in my personal thinking. I am grateful to her, and her colleagues, who provided such a nourishing diet.

I should like to acknowledge permission from the Clarendon Press, Oxford, to print the quotation from R.G. Collingwood's *Principles of Art.*